How to Get More
out of
Holy Communion

St. Peter Julian Eymard

How to Get More out of Holy Communion

SOPHIA INSTITUTE PRESS®
Manchester, New Hampshire

How to Get More out of Holy Communion is an abridged edition of *Holy Communion* (New York: The Sentinel Press, 1940) and contains minor editorial revisions to the original text.

Printed in the United States of America

Jacket design by Lorraine Bilodeau

On the cover is *Christ and the Disciples at Emmaus* (photo copyright © Ali Meyer / CORBIS).

Sophia Institute Press®
Box 5284, Manchester, NH 03108
1-800-888-9344
www.sophiainstitute.com

Imprimi potest: Omer Hébert, S.S.S., *Provincialis*
Nihil obstat: Arthur J. Scanlan, S.T.D., *Censor Librorum*
Imprimatur: Francis J. Spellman, D.D., Archbishop of New York
October 2, 1940

Library of Congress Cataloging-in-Publication Data

Eymard, Pierre Julien, Saint, 1811-1868.
How to get more out of Holy Communion / Peter Julian Eymard. — Abridged ed.
p. cm.
Rev. ed. of: Holy Communion.
ISBN 1-928832-08-3
1. Lord's Supper — Catholic Church. 2. Catholic Church — Doctrines. I. Eymard, Pierre Julien, Saint, 1811-1868. Holy Communion. II. Title.

BX2215.2.E962 2000
264′.02036 — dc21 00-020721

00 01 02 03 04 05 10 9 8 7 6 5 4 3 2

Contents

How to Get More out of Holy Communion

Editor's note: The biblical references in the following pages are based on the Douay-Rheims edition of the Old and New Testaments. Where applicable, biblical quotations have been cross-referenced with the differing names and numeration in the Revised Standard Version, using the following symbol: (RSV =).

Chapter One

Develop the spirit of Communion

"Open thy mouth wide,
and I will fill it."

Psalm 80:11
(RSV = Psalm 81:10)

The love of Jesus Christ reaches its highest perfection and produces the richest harvest of graces in the ineffable union He contracts with the soul in Holy Communion. Therefore, by every desire for goodness, holiness, and perfection that piety, the virtues, and love can inspire in us, we are bound to direct our course toward this union, toward frequent and even daily Communion.

Since we have in Holy Communion the grace, the model, and the practice of all the virtues, all of them finding their exercise in this divine action, we shall profit more by Communion than by all other means of sanctification. But to that end, Holy Communion must become the thought that dominates mind and heart. It must be the aim of all study, of piety, of the virtues. The receiving of Jesus must be the goal as well as the law of life. All our works must converge toward Communion as toward their end and flow from it as from their source.

Let us so live that we may be admitted with profit to frequent and even daily Communion. In a word, let us perfect ourselves in order to receive Communion worthily, and let us live with a constant view to Communion.

But perhaps you will say that your nothingness is overwhelmed by the majesty of God. Ah, but no! That majesty, the celestial and divine majesty which reigns in Heaven, is not present in Holy Communion. Do you not see that Jesus has veiled Himself in order not to frighten you, in order to embolden you to look upon Him and come near to Him?

Or perhaps the sense of your unworthiness keeps you away from this God of all sanctity. It is true that the greatest saint or even the purest of the Cherubim is unworthy to receive the divine Host. But do you not see that Jesus is hiding His virtues, is hiding His very sanctity, to show you His goodness simply and solely? Do you not hear that sweet voice inviting you: "Come unto me"?[1] Do you not feel the nearness of that divine love like a magnet drawing you? After all, it is not your merits that give you your rights, nor is it your virtues that open to you the doors of the Cenacle;[2] it is the love of Jesus.

"But I have so little piety, so little love; how can my soul receive our Lord when it is so lukewarm and therefore so repulsive and so undeserving of His notice?"

Lukewarm? That is but one more reason why you should plunge again and again into this burning furnace. Repulsive? Oh, never, to this good Shepherd, this tender Father, fatherly above all fathers, motherly above all mothers! The more weak and ill you are, the more you need His help. Is not bread the sustenance of both strong and weak?

"But if I have sins on my conscience?" If, after examination, you are not morally certain or positively conscious of any mortal sin, you may go to Holy Communion. If you forgive all

[1] Matt. 11:28.

[2] From the Latin *cenaculum*, or "eating room," often located in the upper story of a house, the Cenacle is the room in which the Last Supper took place.

who have offended you, already your own offenses are forgiven you. And as for your daily negligences, your distractions during prayer, your first movements of impatience, of vanity, of self-love, as likewise for your failure, in your sloth, to put away from you immediately the fire of temptation — bind together all these shoots of Adam's sin and cast them into the furnace of divine love. What love forgives is forgiven indeed.

Ah, do not let yourself be turned away from the Holy Table by vain pretexts! If you will not communicate for your own sake, then communicate instead for Jesus Christ. To communicate for Jesus Christ is to console Him for the neglect to which the majority of men have abandoned Him. It is to confirm His wisdom in instituting this Sacrament of spiritual sustenance. It is to open the riches of the treasures of grace that Jesus Christ has stored up in the Eucharist, only so that He may bestow them upon mankind. Nay, more, it is to give to His sacramental love the overflowing life it desires, to His goodness the happiness of doing good, and to His majesty the glory of bestowing His gifts. By receiving Communion, therefore, you fulfill the glorious purpose of the Holy Eucharist, for if there were no communicants, this fountain would flow in vain, this furnace of love would inflame no hearts, and this King would reign without subjects.

Holy Communion not only gives to the sacramental Jesus the opportunity to satisfy His love; it gives Him a new life that He will consecrate to the glory of His Father. In His state of glory, He can no longer honor the Father with a love free and meritorious. But in Communion, He will enter into man, associate with him, and unite with him. In return, by this wonderful union, the Christian will give members, living and sentient faculties, to the glorified Jesus; he will give Him the liberty that constitutes the merit of virtue. Thus, through Communion, the Christian will be transformed into Jesus Himself, and Jesus will live again in him.

Something divine will then come to pass in the one who communicates; man will labor, and Jesus will give the grace of labor; man will keep the merit, but to Jesus will be the glory. Jesus will be able to say to His Father: "I love Thee, I adore Thee, and I still suffer, living anew in my members."

This is what gives Communion its highest power: it is a second and perpetual incarnation of Jesus Christ. Between Jesus Christ and man, it forms a union of life and love. In a word, it is a second life for Jesus Christ.

Chapter Two

The Eucharist meets your every need

"Thou gavest them bread from Heaven,
having in it the sweetness of every taste."

Cf. Wisdom 16:20

The manna that God sent down every morning into the camp of the Israelites had all sorts of flavors and virtues; it not only restored failing energies and gave vigor of body, but it was a bread of sweetness. The Holy Eucharist, which it prefigures, possesses likewise every virtue. It is a remedy for our spiritual infirmities, strength for our daily weaknesses, and a source of peace, joy, and happiness.

The Eucharist, according to the Council of Trent, is a divine antidote that delivers us from common faults and preserves us from mortal sin. It is a fire that, in an instant, consumes the chaff of our spiritual imperfections.

Holy Communion is the war that God wages in us against our concupiscence and against the Devil, whom our evil passions constantly invite and who, through his connivance with our unruly appetites, holds some part of us in thrall. Did not Jesus say, "Come to me, all you who labor beneath the burden of slavery of your past sins, and I will refresh and deliver you"?[3]

Holy Penance cleanses us from sin, yet, purified though we be, we are left with the marks of our chains, the tendency to fall again. The enemy, although driven out, still keeps his agents within the walls. So Jesus comes to us to destroy the

[3] Cf. Matt. 11:28.

vestiges of our sins, to counteract our evil tendencies, and to prevent the Devil from re-establishing his power over us.

Holy Communion is more than a remedy; it is a force that gives us powerful assistance in attaining goodness, virtue, and holiness.

Certainly it is not easy to acquire a Christian virtue. It means investing ourselves with a quality of Jesus; it is a divine education, a conformation of our ways to those of Jesus. Now, in Holy Communion, Jesus Himself forms His likeness within us. He becomes our own Teacher. By the inspirations of His love, He awakens the gratitude we owe Him as our Benefactor, the desire to resemble Him, a foretaste of the happiness that lies in imitating Him and drawing our life from His.

How attractive the learning of virtue becomes through Communion! How easy is humility when we have seen the God of glory humble Himself so far as to come to a heart so poor, a mind so ignorant, a body so miserable! How easy is kindness when we are moved by the loving-kindness of Jesus in giving Himself to us in the goodness of His Heart!

How beautiful in our sight is our dear neighbor when we see him seated at the same divine banquet, fed with the same Bread of Life, loved so generously by Jesus Christ!

How sweet do penance, self-mortification, and sacrifice become when we have received the crucified Jesus! And with what urgency we feel the need of embracing the life of Him who saved us, of Him who gave us the Holy Eucharist!

The Christian is formed much more quickly in the Cenacle than in any other school. The fact is, all the graces act at once in Communion; beneath the powerful influence of this divine Sun that is within us, penetrating us with His light and His fire, all the virtues of the Savior are reflected in our being. Communion is, in effect, the divine mold of Jesus in our souls and in our bodies.

Hear the words of Jesus: "He who eateth my Body and drinketh my Blood abideth in me, and I in him."[4] So does Jesus live in the communicant, and the communicant in Jesus. It is a joining of two lives, an ineffable union of love, one and the same life in two persons.

Furthermore, Holy Communion is happiness. What is happiness if not the possession of an infinite good, the real and permanent possession of God? Well, such is the divine fruit of Communion.

Communion is also peace. Jesus is the God of peace. "Peace I leave with you; my peace I give unto you,"[5] He said to His Apostles after He had given them Communion — not the troubled and stormy peace of the world, but the peace of God, so sweet that it passes all understanding.[6] With one word, Jesus quiets the tempest; with one glance He scatters and lays low our enemies.

Holy Communion, again, is sweetness. It is the true manna that satisfies all our desires, because it possesses all sweetness. It is the celestial fragrance of the fair Lily of the Valley,[7] which enraptures us in God.

The humble and recollected soul feels in its depths a certain joyous tremor caused by the presence of Jesus Christ; it

[4] John 6:57 (RSV = John 6:56).

[5] John 14:27.

[6] Cf. Phil. 4:7.

[7] Cf. Cant. 2:1 (RSV = Song of Sol. 2:1).

feels itself unfolding beneath the warmth of this Sun of love; it experiences a well-being, an alertness, a sweetness, a force of union, of adhesion to God, that come not from itself. It is aware of Jesus in all its being and looks upon itself as a paradise inhabited by God, where, as in another heavenly court, it may repeat all the praises, thanksgivings, and benedictions sung by the angels and saints to God in glory.

O happy moment of Communion, which makes us forget our exile and its miseries! O sweet repose of the soul on the very Heart of Jesus!

This good Master knows very well that we need to taste the sweetness of love now and then! One cannot be always on the Calvary of suffering, nor in the thick of the battle. The child needs the mother's bosom; the Christian, the Heart of Jesus.

Yes, virtue without Communion is like the strength of the lion; it is the result of combat, of violence; it is hard. If it is to have the gentleness of the lamb, we must drink the Blood of the spotless Lamb; we must eat this honey of the desert.

After all, happiness begets love; we love only that which gives happiness. Seek no farther, then. The Savior has placed this divine happiness neither in the different virtues nor in His other mysteries, but solely within Himself. To taste His joy to the full, we must receive Him as our Food. "Taste and see how sweet is the Lord,"[8] said the prophet. And our Lord Himself said, "He who eateth my Flesh and drinketh my Blood hath everlasting life."[9] And that life everlasting is Heaven; it is sanctity beatified in Jesus Christ.

[8] Cf. Ps. 33:9 (RSV = Ps. 34:8).

[9] John 6:55 (RSV = John 6:54).

Thus the Savior's virtues, the different mysteries of His life, and even of His Passion are but so many roads whose destination is the eucharistic Cenacle. Only there has Jesus made Himself a lasting abode on earth. There we must dwell, there live and die.

Chapter Three

The Bread of Life gives you strength

"I am the Bread of Life."

John 6:35

It was Jesus who adopted the name *Bread of Life*. And what a name! He alone could give it to Himself. An angel charged with naming our Lord would have given Him a title consonant with His attributes, such as Divine Word, or Lord, or the like — but *Bread:* such a name he would never have dared to give to his God!

Bread of Life! Ah, but that is the true name of Jesus; in it is the whole Christ, in His life, in His death, and after His Resurrection. Crushed on the Cross and sifted like flour, He will have after His Resurrection the same properties for our souls as material bread has for our bodies; He will be in truth our Bread of Life.

Material bread nourishes and sustains life. Lest we faint away, we must keep up our strength by taking food, of which bread is the very essential. It is more substantial to our bodies than any other nutriment and sufficient alone for life. The soul, in its natural life, must live forever; it has received that immortality from God. But the life of grace received in Baptism, and regained and renewed in the sacrament of Penance, that life of sanctity, more noble by far than the natural life, cannot be maintained without sustenance; and its principal nutriment is the eucharistic Jesus. The life restored by holy Penance will be brought to fruition in some sort by the Eucharist, which will cleanse us from our affections to sin, will blot out our daily offenses, will give us strength to carry out our good resolutions, and will remove from us the occasions of sin.

The Lord said, "He that eateth my flesh hath life."[10] What life? The life of Jesus Himself. "As the living Father hath sent me, and I live by the Father; so he that eateth me, the same also shall live by me."[11] In fact, food imparts its own substance to him who eats of it. Jesus will not be changed into us; He will transform us into His own image.

Our very body will receive in Communion a pledge of resurrection, and, even in this life, it will be more temperate, more obedient to the soul. It will but take its rest in the tomb, conserving the eucharistic seed, source of a more splendid glory for it in the day of eternal reward.

But we eat not merely to sustain life; we eat to gather as much energy as the work of life demands; it is hardly prudent and certainly insufficient to eat merely in order not to starve. The body must labor, and it will have to expend in its toil not its own substance — which would soon destroy it — but the superfluous strength it has drawn from food. It is a truism that we cannot give what we do not have; therefore, the man condemned to work hard without receiving sufficient food each day will soon lose his strength.

Now, the more we desire to come near to God and live a virtuous life, the more we must expect combat; consequently, we need to gather more and more strength in order not to be vanquished. For all these struggles of the Christian life, the

[10] Cf. John 6:55 (RSV = John 6:54).

[11] John 6:58 (RSV = John 6:57).

Holy Eucharist will give the necessary strength. Without the Eucharist, prayer and piety soon languish. The religious life is nothing but a continual crucifixion of our nature and, of itself, holds no attraction for us. Without strong and gracious help, we do not willingly accept the Cross. Generally speaking, piety without Communion is dead.

Baptism, which bestows life, Confirmation, which increases it, Penance, which restores it — none of these is enough; these sacraments are only preparation for the Eucharist, which is their fruition and their crown.

Jesus said, "Follow me,"[12] but that is difficult; it takes effort and demands the practice of the Christian virtues. We must remember that he alone who abides in our Lord will bear much fruit. And how shall we abide in Him if not by eating His Flesh and drinking His Blood?[13]

Possessing Jesus within us, we are two persons, and the burden, so shared, is light. Therefore did St. Paul say, "I can do all things in Him who strengtheneth me."[14] And He who so strengthened him is the same who lives in us — Christ Jesus.

Whatever its appearance, moreover, bread possesses a certain attraction. The proof is that we never tire of it. Who has ever turned against bread, even when all food seemed tasteless? And where, pray, shall we find substantial sweetness if not in that honeycomb, the Holy Eucharist?

So it follows that piety which is not frequently nourished by Holy Communion has no sweetness; it is not rooted in, nor

[12] Matt. 16:24.

[13] Cf. John 6:57 (RSV = John 6:56).

[14] Phil. 4:13.

animated by, the love of Jesus Christ. It neither attracts us nor appeals to our love. It is harsh, austere, and rude. It would go to God by the way of sacrifice alone — a good way, surely, but how difficult it is not to give way to discouragement! The bow, bent too far, might break. Those who follow this road win much merit, without doubt, but they miss the heart and sweetness of sanctity, which are found only in Jesus.

You want to progress without Communion? But Christian tradition is against you! No longer say the Our Father, since you ask in that prayer for your daily Bread, the Bread you think to do without!

Without Communion, one is constantly in the heat of the battle. One knows only the difficulties in the acquisition of virtue, not the sweetness of its practice — the joy of working, not simply for oneself and moved solely by the hope of reward, but purely for the glory of God, from love of Him, from affection, like little children. He who receives Communion finds it easy to understand that having received much, he must give a great deal in return. That is piety — intelligent, filial, and loving piety. Besides, even in the severest trials, Communion makes the soul happy, filling it with a tender and loving joy.

The height of perfection is to remain united with God in the midst of the most violent interior temptations, and it is when you are most tempted that God most loves you. Yet, in order that these storms may not overwhelm you, learn to return frequently to the divine fountainhead to renew your strength and to purify yourself more and more in that torrent of grace and love.

Receive Communion therefore! Eat the Bread of Life if you wish to live well, if you wish to obtain sufficient strength for the Christian combat, if you wish to possess happiness even in the thick of misfortune.

The Holy Eucharist is the Bread of the weak and of the strong. To the weak, clearly, it is necessary; but to the strong likewise, since they bear their treasure in fragile vessels and are threatened on every hand by desperate enemies. Let us, then, take care that we have a guard, a sure escort, fortifying food for our journey; this will Jesus be, our Bread of Life.

Chapter Four

Your spirit will find joy in Communion

"My spirit hath rejoiced
in God my Savior."

Luke 1:47

God desired to nourish our spirit, so He gave it His Bread, the Eucharist, announced by Holy Scripture: "He will feed them with the Bread of life and understanding."[15]

Now, there are no greater joys on earth than the joys of the spirit. Contentment of heart is less lasting because it is based on feeling, and feeling is apt to be inconstant. True joy is of the spirit and consists in the quiet knowledge of the truth.

The light-minded and coarse of soul enjoy nothing spiritually. Even pious souls that lack recollection will never experience spiritual joys. Frivolity of spirit is the greatest obstacle to the reign of God in the soul. If you wish to taste the sweetness of God and enjoy His presence, you must lead a life of recollection and prayer. Even so, your meditations will never yield true happiness if they are not based on Communion, but will only leave you with the sense of perpetual sacrifice.

Jesus Christ exercised the prerogative that was His to give us experience of true joy through Himself alone. The soul that only seldom receives Communion gives God no opportunity to dwell in it in a completely efficacious way. The one, on the contrary, that receives Him frequently will be longer and more often in His presence and, seeing Him and contemplating

[15] Cf. Ecclus. 15:3.

Him freely, will learn to know Him well and will end by enjoying Him.

In Communion, we enjoy our Lord in our Lord Himself. It is then that we have our most intimate communion with Him — a communion from which we gain a true and profound knowledge of what He is. It is then that Jesus manifests Himself to us most clearly. Faith is a light; Communion is at once light and feeling.

This manifestation of Jesus through Communion enlightens the mind and gives it a special aptitude for discerning more and more clearly the things of God. Just as the elect receive the power to contemplate the being and the majesty of God without being blinded, likewise Jesus, in Communion, increases our ability to know Him, and to such an extent that there is a vast difference in a person before and after Communion.

Take a child before his First Communion; he understands his catechism in the literal sense, word for word. But after Communion, his mind is, as it were, transformed; the child understands then, and feels, and is eager to know more about Jesus Christ. He is fortified and disposed to hear whatever truths you teach.

Can you explain this phenomenon? Before Communion, you hear about Jesus Christ and you know Him; you are told of His Cross, of His suffering. Doubtless you are affected and are even touched with compassion. But let these same truths be presented to you after you have received Communion, and oh, how much more deeply your soul is moved! It cannot hear enough; it understands much more perfectly. Before Communion, you contemplate Jesus outside you; now you contemplate Him within you, with His own eyes!

It is the mystery of Emmaus re-enacted. When Jesus taught the two disciples along the way, explaining the Scriptures to them, their faith still wavered, although they felt inwardly some mysterious emotion. But by their participating in the breaking of the bread, immediately their eyes were opened, and their hearts were ready to burst with joy.[16] The voice of Jesus had not sufficed to reveal His presence to them. They had to feel His Heart; they had to be fed with the Bread of understanding!

Second, this joy of spirit, this manifestation of Himself that Jesus gives us by Communion, awakens in us a hunger for God. This divine hunger draws us into the sweetness of His Heart, into the sanctuary of His Spirit. More by impression than by reason, it gives us knowledge of Him. It gives us a powerful attraction to the Eucharist and everything connected with it and enables us to enter with ease into Jesus Christ.

This ease, this attraction, mysterious to some extent, is the special grace of Communion. It is the spirit of kinship with God. From where, do you think, does that similarity of feeling, of acting, of morals in a family come, if not from family spirit, from family love, which unites all members in mutual affection? Such is the bond of earthly kinship.

Through Communion, we gain entrance into the love, into the Heart, of our Lord; we catch the spirit of His love, His own understanding, His own judgment. Is not the first grace of Communion, in fact, a grace of recollection that enables us to penetrate into Jesus Christ and commune intimately with Him? Yes, intimately. One who does not receive Communion

[16] Cf. Luke 24:13-32.

knows, by faith, only the vesture, the outward appearance of our Lord. We can know Jesus Christ well only by receiving Him, just as we perceive the sweetness of honey only by tasting it. We can say, then, with a great saint, "I am more convinced of the truth of Jesus Christ, of His existence, of His perfections by a single Communion than I could be by all the reasoning in the world."

Such is the brevity of this life that, if we had to arrive at the knowledge of truth in general, and of divine truth in particular, only by the proofs of reason, be well assured we would know very few truths. But it is God's will that much of our knowledge should come by intuition. He has endowed us with an instinct by which, without the faculty of reason, we are able to distinguish good from evil, truth from falsehood. He has given us natural inclinations and antipathies. Thus, in our efforts to know our Lord, we first feel His goodness, and then we arrive at His other qualities, more by contemplation, by sight, and by instinct than by reason.

A great many people habitually make the mistake of talking too much in their thanksgiving after Communion, that highest of prayers. By overmuch speaking, they render their Communion ineffective.

Listen to our Lord a little after Communion. This is not the time to seek, but to enjoy. This is the time when God makes Himself known through Himself: "And they shall all be taught of God."[17] How does a mother teach her little child what endless love and tenderness she has for him? She is content to show by her devotion that she loves him. God does the same

[17] John 6:45.

in Communion. Remember that one who does not receive Communion will never know the Heart of our Lord or the magnitude of His love. The heart makes itself known through itself alone; we must feel it beating.

Sometimes you have no experience of spiritual joy in Communion. Wait. Although the Sun is hidden, it is within you; you will feel it when you need to — be sure of that. What am I saying? Already you feel it! Are you not at peace? Are you not desirous of glorifying God more than ever? And what is that but the throbbing of the Heart of our Lord within you?

Lastly, the manifestation of our Lord in Communion makes His presence and His conversation indispensable to the soul. The soul that has known Jesus Christ and has enjoyed Him takes pleasure in nothing else. Creatures leave it cold and indifferent because it compares them with Him. God has left in the soul a need that no person, no creature, can ever satisfy.

Moreover, the soul feels a constant desire for Jesus and for His glory. Ever onward, without pausing to enjoy a moment's rest: that is its motto. Its only longing is for Jesus, who leads it from clarity to clarity. Our Lord being inexhaustible, whoever receives Him can neither be sated nor exhaust Him, but desires only to plunge deeper and deeper into the abysses of His love.

Oh, come and enjoy our Lord often in Communion, if you wish truly to understand Him!

"Beware of abusing this privilege," someone will say. Do the elect go to excess in their enjoyment of God? No! They never enjoy Him too much. Taste the Lord, and you will see. After you have received Communion, you will understand.

How sad that people will not believe us! They wish to judge of God only by faith. But taste first; afterward you shall judge. And if the incredulous would but prepare themselves to receive Jesus Christ worthily, they would understand sooner and better than by any amount of persuasion and reasoning. Besides, the ignorant person who receives well knows more about it than the savant, however learned, who does not go to Communion.

To summarize briefly, I say that the intelligence finds its supreme happiness in Communion and that, the more often one receives, the happier one is spiritually. God is the only source of happiness; happiness is in Him alone, and He has reserved the right to bestow it through Himself. And well it is for us that we must go to God Himself to find happiness! In this way, we do not devote ourselves to creatures or find in them our highest good. Happiness is not even in the bestowal of the priest. He gives you a share in the fruits of the Redemption, cleanses you from your sins, and gives you the peace of a clear conscience; but happiness and joy he cannot give you.

Mary herself, who is the Mother of Mercy, will lead you back to the right way and will appease the anger of her Son, whom you have offended; but God alone will give you joy and happiness. The angel said to the shepherds, "I bring you good tidings of great joy: He who is its cause and its source, your Savior and God, is born to you."[18]

Oh, come, let us rejoice! This Savior is still on the altar waiting to flood our hearts, upon His entrance therein, with as much joy and happiness as we are able to bear, in anticipation of the unspeakable and everlasting delights of the homeland of Heaven.

[18] Cf. Luke 2:11.

Chapter Five

Communion reveals God's love for you

"I will write my
law in their heart."

Cf. Jeremiah 31:33

Not only does Communion enlighten our mind by a special grace, revealing to us, by impression rather than by reason, all that our Lord is, but it is also, and above all, the revelation to our heart of the law of love.

The Eucharist is the sacrament of love par excellence. Certainly the other sacraments are proofs of God's love for us; they are gifts of God. But in the Eucharist, we receive the Author of every gift, God Himself. So it is in Communion especially that we learn to know the law of love that our Lord came to reveal. There we receive the special grace of love. There, finally, more than anywhere else, we acquire the practice, the virtue, of love.

First of all, what is love? It is a *gift*. That is why the Holy Spirit, who, as love, proceeds from the First and Second Persons of the Most Holy Trinity, is truly the *Gift*.

How do we recognize love? By what it gives. See what our Lord gives us in the Eucharist: all His graces and all His possessions are for us; His gift is Himself, the source of every gift. Communion gives us participation in the merits of all His life and obliges us to recognize the love that God has for us, because, in Communion, we receive the whole and perfect gift.

How did you begin to love your mother? Sleeping within you, without sign of life, was a seed, an instinct, of love. Your mother's love awakened it; she cared for you, suffered for you, fed you with her body. By this generous gift you recognized her love. Well then! Our Lord, by giving Himself entirely to you, and to you in particular, proves to you invincibly that He loves you personally with an infinite love. He is in the Eucharist for you and entirely for you. Others enjoy Him also, to be sure, but in the same way that they benefit from the sun without preventing you from enjoying its rays as much as you wish.

Ah, such is this law of love engraved in our hearts by God Himself in Communion! In olden times, God wrote His law on tables of stone, but the New Law He has written in our hearts, with letters of fire. Oh, whoever does not know the Eucharist does not know the love of God! At most, he knows certain effects of it, as the beggar recognizes the generosity of the rich man from the few coins he receives from him. But in Communion, the Christian sees himself loved with all of God's power to love, with all of Himself. Therefore, if you would really know God's love for you, receive the Eucharist, and then look within you. You have no need to seek elsewhere for further proofs.

Communion gives us the grace of love. In order to love Jesus Christ as a Friend we need a special grace. Jesus, in coming to us, brings this grace at the same time that He places the object of it — that is, Himself — in our soul. Our Lord did not ask His disciples before the Last Supper to love Him as He had loved them; He did not yet say to them, "Abide in my love."[19] That was too hard for them then; they would not have understood. But after the Last Supper, He no longer says simply, "Love God; love your neighbor," but, "Love me as a brother,

[19] John 15:9.

intimately, with a love that is your life and the law of your life." "I will not now call you servants . . . but friends."[20]

If you do not receive Communion, you can love our Lord as your Creator, your Redeemer, and your Rewarder, but you will never see in Him your Friend. Friendship is based on union, on a certain equality, two things that are found with God only in the Eucharist. Who, I ask you, would dare call himself the friend of God and believe himself worthy of His particular affection? A servant would insult his master in presuming to treat him as a friend; he must wait until his master grants him the right by first calling him by that name.

But when God Himself has come under our roof; when He has come to share with us His life, His possessions, and His merits; when He has thus made the first advances, we no longer presume, but with reason call Him our Friend. So, after the Last Supper, our Lord tells His Apostles, "I will not now call you servants. I call you friends. You are my friends, because all things whatsoever I have received of my Father I have given to you; you are my friends, because to you I have confided the secret of my majesty."

He will do even more; He will appear to Mary Magdalene and say to her, "Go to my brethren."[21] What? His brethren? Can there be a higher title? Yet the Apostles had received Communion only once! What will it be for those who, like us, have received Him so often?

Will anyone be afraid now to love our Lord with the tenderest affection? It is well to tremble before Communion,

[20] John 15:15.

[21] John 20:17.

thinking of what you are and of Him you are about to receive; you need His mercy then. But afterward, rejoice! There is no longer room for fear; even humility must make way for gladness. See how joyous Zacchaeus is when our Lord accepts his hospitality! But see, too, how his devotion is fired by this kind reception; he is ready to make every sacrifice and to atone over and over for all his sins.[22]

The more you receive Communion, the more will your love be enkindled, your heart enlarged; your affection will become more ardent and tender as the intensity of this divine fire increases. Jesus bestows upon us the grace of His love. He comes Himself to kindle this flame of love in our hearts. He feeds it by His frequent visits until it becomes a consuming fire. This is in truth the "live coal which sets us on fire."[23] And if we so will, this fire will never go out, for it is fed not by us but by Jesus Christ Himself, who gives to it His force and action. Do not extinguish it by willful sin, and it will burn on forever.

Come often, every day if necessary, to this divine Furnace to increase the tiny flame in your hearts! Do you think your fire will continue to burn if you do not feed it?

Communion makes us practice the virtue of love. True and perfect love finds its full expression only in Communion. If a fire cannot spread, it goes out. So our Lord, wishing us to love Him and knowing how incapable of it we are of ourselves, fills us with His own love; He Himself comes and loves in us. We, then, work on a divine object. There is no gradual passage or transition; we are simultaneously in the grace and in the

[22] Cf. Luke 19:2-8.

[23] St. John Chrysostom (c. 347-407), Bishop of Constantinople.

object of love. That is why our best and most fervent acts of love are made during our thanksgiving; we are nearer then to Him who forms them. Pour out your heart to our Lord at this time. Love Him tenderly.

Do not try so hard to make this or that act of virtue. Let our Lord grow within you. Enter into partnership with Him; let Him be the capital in your soul's traffic, and your gains will be doubled with the doubling of your spiritual funds. Working with and by our Lord, you will gain a greater benefit than if you tried to increase your virtues simply by multiplied acts.

Receive our Lord, and keep Him as long as you can. Make plenty of room for Him within you. To let Jesus Christ increase in one's soul is the most perfect act of love. Certainly, penitent and suffering love is good and meritorious; but the heart is repressed by it, weighed down beneath the thought of the continual sacrifices it must bear. This way, on the contrary, the heart expands, opens fully and freely; it shows its happiness.

For one who does not receive Communion, these words have no meaning; but let him plunge into this divine fire, and he will understand.

No, it is not enough simply to believe in the Holy Eucharist; we must also obey the laws it prescribes. Since the Eucharist is above all the Sacrament of love, our Lord desires us to share in that love and draw inspiration therefrom. So come to Jesus out of love for Him! We must come humbly, to be sure; but let love, or at least the longing to love, be our ruling motive. Let us desire to pour out our heart in His Heart; let us give evidence to Him of our tenderness and affection. Then we shall know what depths of love are in the adorable Eucharist.

Chapter Six

Communion prepares you for Heaven

"I will draw them with the cords of Adam, with the bands of love."

Osee 11:4
(RSV = Hosea 11:4)

It is certain that the Eucharist gives to the soul that worthily receives it an experience of happiness, of delights found nowhere but in that Sacrament.

Why does God so greatly desire to communicate His sweetness to us? Because there is only one thing that can attach us to Him, and that is His goodness.

There is sympathy of feeling only between equals. The powerful meet envy on every side. Kings have no friends unless they stoop to seek them. As for us, we tremble before the power of God, and even His sanctity does not bespeak our affection; it is for His goodness that we love Him. We know that He wishes to save us, that He descends even to our lowliness. The mysteries of our Lord's life that make us love Him most are those in which He shows us the most tender and lavish goodness. Only God's goodness can make us love Him steadfastly.

When do we see our Lord most lovingly adored in His earthly life? The Wise Men adored Him as He lay in the manger because He was so lovable there. The man born blind was so touched by the love Jesus had shown Him that he wanted to follow Him. When Magdalene heard that her sins were forgiven her, a fire was kindled in her heart that would never be extinguished; our Lord had shown her such goodness!

Yes, truly, we are captivated only by goodness. Therefore, the Church, which understands divine things so well, says in one of her prayers, "O God, whose nature is goodness." But are not all the other attributes of God equally of His essence? He is perfect in all, and all are equal, doubtless; but here below, for us humans, the nature of God is goodness.

This being so, it follows that we must love our Lord most in the greatest manifestation of His goodness. And is not His goodness most strikingly manifested in the Holy Eucharist, in Communion? Says the Council of Trent, "In this Sacrament, God has poured forth bountifully the riches of His love."[24] It is the very culmination of His love. God can give us no greater gift than Himself. By means of Communion, we receive Jesus Christ as God and as Man, together with the merits of His mortal life and all its states, with the Redemption and all its fruits, even the pledge of future glory. We receive the greatest sum of happiness God can give on earth.

And we feel this happiness. It is necessary that we should enjoy it. Without the sweetness of union with God, it is very difficult, generally speaking, to remain in the state of grace.

The sacrament of Penance restores the life of grace in us, heals us. But it is a violent remedy, a victory dearly bought, which leaves us weary with battle. And although this sacrament restores life to the soul, it will be insufficient to maintain that life for long; if we go no further, we shall be no more than convalescents.

What do we need in order to regain the fullness of life and strength? What but Communion, that balm, that sweet and

[24] Session 13, ch. 2.

healing warmth, the milk of our Lord, as the prophet says?[25] After Holy Penance, the Eucharist makes our peace complete. We need to hear that word of encouragement from the lips of our Savior Himself: "Go in peace, and sin no more"[26] — that word which, escaping from His Heart, falls like a heavenly dew upon our own bruised and ulcered heart.

Communion gives us perseverance to the end. Nothing is so discouraging as a long road ahead of us, and it is the common feeling of beginners to say, "I can never hold out so long!" If you wish final perseverance, receive our Lord!

One who rarely receives Communion may keep himself in a state of grace for Heaven; but how far away Heaven is, and what faith he must have to keep his eyes fixed constantly on so distant a hope! The life of faith is, then, but one continual sacrifice, a battle waged without truce or refreshment and with no effective, supporting force. One who rarely receives Communion is like a traveler far from his native land; the long road consumes his strength and brings him to the point of despair.

Also, if one receives Communion only infrequently, it is difficult to keep in the state of grace for any length of time. Although one may do so, the soul will no longer possess its pristine beauty and purity; the dust of the highway will have clung to it and dimmed its splendor. So experience teaches.

But if we often receive Communion, oh, how much easier it is to preserve grace in its first purity! We no longer have to guard it carefully for a far-distant goal, but simply for tomorrow, for today. We know it is the garb of honor that admits us

[25] Cf. Isa. 66:11.

[26] Cf. John 8:11.

to the Feast. Therefore, we avoid sin out of love, so that we may not be deprived of Holy Communion. Thus, Communion becomes a sure defense against sin and enables us to overcome it easily to the end of our life. I am speaking of willful sin.

How could the soul that communicates every day and to which Communion means so much yield to temptation? It knows that sin would deprive it of what it so greatly desires. The thought of its next Communion rises before the soul, strengthens it, encourages it, and prevents it from falling.

I confess that the state of grace is incomprehensible to me unless it is supported by Communion.

Besides, that is the intention of the Church which, through the Council of Trent, encourages us to receive Communion daily. The Eucharist, received infrequently, would be but an extraordinary nutriment. Where, then, is our regular food, the daily bread we need to give us strength? What is to nourish within us the love of God, which forms the life and merit of the Christian virtues? Only Communion.

Communion makes the state of grace desirable and assures its permanence, because Jesus Christ becomes its direct and immediate end. Communion gives us constancy in virtue and ease in its practice by nourishing the love of God in us; it makes virtue sweet and inviting by giving it a living and active object.

Let us prepare for Paradise by Communion. There the blessed receive our Lord perpetually, living by His knowledge and His love. Let us receive Him well here below so that we may be ready to do the same in Heaven. Communion, received frequently and with the requisite dispositions, is the surest pledge of eternal salvation.

Chapter Seven

Communion sustains and refreshes you

"Except you eat the Flesh of the Son of Man, and drink His Blood, you shall not have life in you."

John 6:54
(RSV = John 6:53)

In the opinion of the Fathers of the Church, the Incarnation is a second creation. In Jesus Christ we have been created anew, rehabilitated; our life and our dignity have been restored to us.

What has been said of the Incarnation can be said likewise of the Eucharist, which is but the extension thereof. Let us see how in the Eucharist we find again the divine life that Original Sin had destroyed in humanity. Jesus Christ said, "Except you eat the Flesh of the Son of Man, and drink His Blood, you shall not have life in you. He that eateth my Flesh and drinketh my Blood hath everlasting life."[27] But does not Baptism, which makes us children of God, give us this divine life? Does not the sacrament of Penance restore it to us when we have had the misfortune to lose it by sin? What, then, is the meaning of these words that our Lord so solemnly emphasizes? Is there a contradiction here in Catholic doctrine? Certainly not.

The Eucharist is the sacrament of life because it gives us life in its full development, in its perfection. The day-old infant has life, doubtless; likewise the enfeebled person who is just recovering from an illness; but leave the former without care and the latter without the strengthening remedies and food of convalescence, and it will not be long before the one

[27] John 6:54-55 (RSV = John 6:53-54).

has lost the life that had hardly begun for him, and the other has relapsed into a worse condition than before.

Baptism and Penance, which give us life, are not sufficient to maintain it. Thus, our Lord, after raising the daughter of Jairus to life, orders that she be given food to eat.[28] Life and the food that sustains it are inseparable. If we wish not to grow weaker and weaker, we must receive the Bread of Heaven. Certainly we can win merit and can labor for Heaven from the moment we enter into the state of grace. In order, however, to keep up our efforts for long, we must take this food of the strong. By no other means can we obtain sufficient strength to endure the hard daily struggle.

However good and necessary prayer is, it will weary you, and you will end by neglecting it unless you are supported in it by Communion.

In order to live the life of penance, in order to progress in this narrow and painful path of self-mortification, we need a divine impulsion — no other than the oft-renewed presence of Jesus Christ in our heart.

The example of the anchorites living in the depths of the desert might seem to contradict this assertion, but, you must know, they went every Sunday to their monastery to receive Communion. And they needed it more than others if they were to progress in their holy calling. For I advance it as a principle that the more one desires to live a pure and holy life, the greater is one's need and the more urgent the obligation to receive Communion frequently. Such a life calls for more sacrifice, and therefore one needs more strength.

[28] Mark 5:42-43.

Communion sustains and refreshes you

You have to work a great deal? Then eat in proportion. Look upon Communion simply as the source of your sustenance and strength. It is not an exalted and arduous act of virtue, nor is it offered to you as a recompense for your virtues. You must receive Communion, not because you are holy, but because you wish to become so. That is the rule. Go to Communion because you are weak and overburdened by the labors of the Christian life. See how Jesus Christ calls you to Communion: "Come to me, all you that labor and are burdened, and I will refresh you."[29]

If at times Communion does not give us that rest and refreshment, it is because we make of it a difficult act of virtue. We exert ourselves to the utmost in it, making countless exhausting acts — in short, laboring when we should be taking repose and nourishment.

Receive our Lord, and be at peace. Why all this agitation? You do not go to a banquet to transact business. Enjoy this celestial Food, then, and since you are receiving the Bread of angels, give yourself, like the angels, to contemplation for a while. You do not take the time to taste our Lord, and then you withdraw full of anxiety over having felt nothing! Follow in spirit the example of the Carthusians, who lie prostrate at the foot of the altar throughout the time of their thanksgiving.

Good people will often say, "My Communions do not profit me, for I do not feel them." That is a wrong conclusion. They do profit, since their souls have life. A good Communion does not necessarily call forth heroic acts of virtue or such sacrifices as are most repugnant to you. The Eucharist is

[29] Matt. 11:28.

sweetness and strength. Thus it is represented throughout the Old Testament. Now it is a bread containing all sweetness.[30] Again, it is a mysterious bread that, offered to the discouraged Elijah, gives him strength to continue his journey.[31] In another instance, it is the refreshing cloud that cools the desert by day, the fire that gives light and warmth by night.[32] Such is the Holy Eucharist. If you are weak, it strengthens you; if you are weary, it gives you rest. It is essentially a help proportioned to each one's need.

The conclusion of all we have just said is this: If you wish to be strong and enjoy that fullness of life of which you stand in need, go to Communion. Our Lord, speaking of the Eucharist, said, "If any man eat of this Bread, he shall live forever."[33] He will have an abundance of life — not a mere trickle, but the source, the river, the ocean, of life; a life that is nourished by itself and is ours forever, provided we will receive it. It is the life of Jesus Christ Himself, a life of love that is ours as long as we love; and whoever lives by thanksgiving has within him the true life of Jesus. Corporally our Lord remains in our hearts only a little while after Communion, but the effects of Communion remain; His Spirit abides with us. Like a capsule enveloping a medicine, the Sacred Species dissolve and disappear, leaving a divine remedy to produce its beneficial effects in our being.

I cannot conceive how anyone can keep his purity in this world or progress at all without Communion. There are pious

[30] Cf. Wisd. 16:20.

[31] Cf. 3 Kings 19:4-8 (RSV = 1 Kings 19:4-8).

[32] Cf. Exod. 13:21.

[33] John 6:52 (RSV = John 6:51).

persons who say, "I do not need frequent Communion; I am always at peace." Too much so! This complete calm presages storm. Oh, do not admire your little virtues. Put no faith in this peace. Do not place so much confidence in yourself. Aim to progress, and, with that in view, receive Communion often.

Alas, many excuse themselves from frequent Communion under pretext of fatigue, indisposition, or lack of devotion. It is a snare of the Devil, and if you surrender on one occasion, he will beset you every day with the same pretexts. To act thus is to be discourteous and rude to our Lord, to insult Him. You will be called to account for this neglected Communion, as the lazy servant in the Gospel was for the buried talent.[34]

Come, then! Come to renew your strength often at the Holy Table. And may the powerful and active life you find there increase constantly within you until God transforms it into the life of eternal blessedness.

[34] Cf. Matt. 25:24-28.

Chapter Eight

Through Communion, you regain your dignity

"O God, who, in creating human nature, didst marvelously ennoble it, and hast still more marvelously renewed it . . ."

The Missal

Jesus instituted the Eucharist in order to reinstate the human race in its first dignity. Man was degraded, debased, by Original Sin. He forgot his celestial origin, lost his honor as king of creation, and became like the beasts he was meant to govern. Cast into their midst, he was eluded by the weak or attacked by the strong, sin having made him who was their master their mortal enemy. He remained by his nature their king, but a king dethroned.

Driven from his kingdom, man was to become even more shamefully degraded by willful sin, was to descend to the level of the brute. Thus idolaters felt themselves, by sin, so near to the beast that they gave it divine honors, prostrating themselves before vile animals. Man was so aware of his degradation that he felt a secret need of adoring creatures that would not put him to shame. From his Creator, however, he fled, not daring to meet His glance.

But behold the divine plan, how marvelous it is! God knew the unbearable shame man would feel if, from the depths of his misery, he were to be called directly into His presence. So God would find a way to rehabilitate man, to restore his honor. And as food and clothing are the two things most apt to bring men together among themselves, God would give to man a celestial raiment and a divine nutriment. Thus man would be restored to his former dignity. Baptism will purify the child of Adam; the virtues of Jesus Christ will adorn him; the Eucharist will sanctify him. Surrounded by so many honors, man will feel his dignity increase.

And in fact, Jesus Christ clothes the priest anew in His Body, as Tertullian said.[35] The priest is another Christ; he lives on Christ; our Lord's will is his; he is our Lord living still. And all the faithful who receive Communion share in this privilege. This body, which has received Communion, which has been united to Jesus Christ, is unspeakably venerable. Indeed, one might even be tempted to cast oneself down in adoration before the communicant! Why does the Church venerate so devoutly the relics of the saints if not because those saints received Jesus Christ, because their members were incorporated in Jesus Christ, were His own members?

I will go even further and affirm that by Communion we are raised above the angels, if not in nature, at least in honor. In receiving our Lord, do we not become His brethren, other Christs? The angels are only His ministers. When we have received Him in Communion, oh, with what veneration they gather round us, what honor they show us! In this respect, Communion enhances our worth even beyond what we would have possessed without Original Sin. Innocent, we would have been forever below the angels; regenerated and having become, through the Eucharist, of the same blood with Jesus Christ, we are given the right to occupy a higher throne in Heaven than the celestial spirits. And the more we receive Communion,

[35] Tertullian (c. 160-c. 225; African Church Father), *On Monogamy*, ch. 7.

the more resplendent will be our heavenly glory; each Communion will increase the splendor of our crown.

But, humanly speaking, why do certain persons — priests, for instance — inspire in us at first sight a kind of religious respect? Ah, why, but that we recognize Jesus Christ in them; why, but that Jesus Christ is exhaled from the depths of their heart and from all their person, as the fragrance of a violet pervades the air about it! Even more, it seems to me that if our Lord did not set bounds to His glory in His communicants, they would shine like the sun. In order to preserve their humility, He hides His splendor; enough of it still gleams through. The proximity of a saint calms us and does us good.

And now, consider this: every soul has the mission to save other souls on this earth; but to fulfill this duty, a certain authority is necessary — an authority that is commensurate with the end in view. The one source of this moral authority is Communion; no one can resist a person in whom Jesus Christ dwells and who, by his words and actions, makes us aware of this divine presence. Although a priest who only infrequently celebrates Mass has this mission like other priests, he will never possess the authority that belongs to his mission. The ascendancy over hearts that attracts and converts them comes only from God.

It is not hard to obey the saints, because they come nearer to being a true likeness of Jesus Christ; the very animals obey them. If the saints converted entire kingdoms and peoples, it was not by their own strength but by our Lord, whom they had received and who broke from their hearts like an ardent flame. Ah, but the saints knew how to receive Jesus, how to keep Him, and how to make use of Him for the glory of His Father!

Thus, man is certainly rehabilitated in his dignity by Communion. *O felix culpa!*[36] Yes, happy fault! Degraded as you are, clothed in the skins of beasts as punishment for your pride, put on now our Lord Jesus Christ. Since, in human society, it is dress that commands in greater or lesser degree the world's respect, since the badges of dignity are worn outwardly, put on Jesus Christ. Wearing this garment of glory, you will be honored and deserving of honor. You will have authority with others, an authority both respected and loved, the only kind that can be of benefit. Zacchaeus, despised as a publican, had only to receive Jesus, and immediately our Lord proclaimed him a son of Abraham and silenced his slanderers.[37] And you — you are ennobled by Communion, and your house, to which you bear Jesus Christ, is worthy of honor and respect.

So is our dignity re-established. I admit we are not reinstated in the earthly paradise. But, oh, let that paradise be lost forever! The Eucharist is the true paradise, the delightful garden wherein God tarries in sweet converse with the faithful soul. If, in exchange for my present condition, I were offered that earthly Eden, I would refuse. Yes, in order to keep the Eucharist, I would refuse in spite of my miseries. After all, these miseries are not sins! And by the help of a Bread so substantial, they are easily endured. When one loves, there is no fatigue — or if there is, even that is loved.

[36] "O happy fault [that merited so great a Redeemer]!" St. Thomas Aquinas (c. 1225-1274; Dominican philosopher and theologian), *Summa Theologica*, III, Q. 1, art. 3.

[37] Luke 19:9.

Chapter Nine

In Communion, you receive Christ as a friend

"Say to the fainthearted:
Take courage and fear not."

Isaiah 35:4

Man, having sinned, felt an instinctive fear of God. Immediately after yielding to the tempter, he dared not answer the voice of His Creator but hid himself and fled from His visage.

This sensation of fear is so natural to us when we have done wrong that even a child, in spite of his mother's tenderness, hesitates to go near her when he has disobeyed her. The criminal fleeing from human justice is so possessed with fear that it is written in his face and may even reveal his guilt.

Fear before God is the same, and greater still. You think a certain sinner is hardened and continues in sin simply from pride? No! He is afraid of God; and the greater his sin, the more afraid he is. He may sink to the very depths of iniquity, perpetrate crime after crime; he only gives further proof of his fear.

What is despair but the false conviction that one will not be forgiven and is destined to fall into the hands of an inexorable Judge? People who refuse to come to church are afraid of our Lord. If they are forced to come, they are embarrassed and nervous. The sinner is afraid of himself; he cannot live with his own heart and conscience; he frightens himself! That is why he seeks distraction; he is fleeing from himself.

Sacred Scripture shows us this fear so dominant in mankind that even the holiest persons trembled if God appeared to them or spoke to them in the form of an angel. The holy

Virgin herself, pure as she was, trembled in the presence of the angel of God. Fear dominated the human race.

God took four thousand years to prepare the reconciliation of man, which was to be perfected only in the Eucharist. The Incarnation greatly advanced this work of regaining man's confidence, but it was not enough. For thirty-three years only, Jesus gave evidence to us of His goodness, and we may say that if He had deprived us of His presence after this short period of time, we would be as subject to fear as were the Jews before His advent. Could the Incarnation, work of salvation though it was and a sublime testimonial of the love and power of God, suffice to establish the confidence of friendship between the Creator and His creature? No, friendship demands constant personal communion.

Therefore, our Lord instituted the Most Holy Eucharist. By means of this sacrament, He is in our thought, in us, with us, beside us, continuing and perfecting His work of making us His intimates and friends. Hiding His glory, He comes to us in the incognito of friendship, just as if a king were to assume the guise of a poor man and, seating himself at his table, say to him, "I belong to your family; treat me as one of you." Yet Jesus Christ does even more; He comes to us under the appearance of bread. Who can be afraid of a grain of wheat? Could God find a better way to veil His majesty?

See how easy and delightful communion with our Lord now becomes. Because Jesus Christ is hidden in the Eucharist, you can come near to Him and hear His divine promise. Otherwise, one word from Him would make the world tremble with terror, as on Mount Sinai. One word of love would inflame and consume us, one word of menace annihilate us.

As for imitating His virtues, if Jesus did not veil them in the Eucharist, if He did not put them, so to speak, within our reach, we would despair of attaining to them. But hiding them, seeming to be without life and obeying entirely as if He were only inanimate matter, He encourages us to follow His example. For the same reason, a mother hesitates in her speech and takes tiny steps in teaching her child to talk and walk.

The Eucharist, we may say, is Jesus establishing intimacy between man and God. But the mysteries of the close union Jesus forms with us in Communion! How to describe them? Friendship presupposes union, for without union, perfect confidence cannot exist. Jesus wishes to be united to each of us individually. Moses, with holy audacity, said to God, "Show me Thy glory."[38] And God, although He refused at first, could not resist in the end the confidence with which Moses pleaded and insisted. However, lest Moses should be consumed by the splendor of His glory, God ordered him to stand afar off and then only passed before him. Moses saw but a single ray of the divine Majesty, and, for the rest of his life, his face shone with the dazzling reflection of it.

The glory of Jesus in the Eucharist, if revealed to us, would make us like Moses. But would there be friendship and intimacy? Moses, dazed with glory, was scarcely desirous of speaking or opening his heart! Yet Jesus insists on our friendship. He wishes us to treat Him as our Friend, and to that end, He takes the appearance of bread. No one is frightened; all think they see what has been familiar to them from their childhood:

[38] Exod. 33:18.

bread. All are encouraged, then, to open their hearts. Our Lord takes us unawares.

Zacchaeus had not presumed to wish to speak with our Lord. He simply desired to see Him. Jesus takes him by surprise and calls him by his name. Zacchaeus obeys and finds himself completely changed by so much love. He no longer remembers that he has been only a miserable sinner. No, after an act of sincere humility, he receives Jesus in his house and, without fear, rejoices in the sweetness of His presence.

If Jesus sent an angel to announce Communion and bring it to us instead of coming in the hidden way He does, we would tremble with fear a long time beforehand. But no, in order that we may enjoy the happiness that is ours in Communion, it is necessary that we be taken unawares, and we are. Our eyes see only frail appearances, a lowly form. That is the grace of graces. If it were not for that, we would be too greatly agitated in receiving Communion.

It is good to be moved, but not to be troubled. Our emotion causes us to think more of Him whom we are about to receive and less of our own unworthiness.

And when our Lord is within us, what shall we do but rejoice? By His goodness, we are sheltered from the splendor of His sanctity and are made to forget His power, His glory, and His grandeur. Let us, then, rejoice in this wondrous contrivance of God for us. By the Eucharist, God is present to us; by Communion, we enter into intimacy with Him.

Oh, yes, happy fault! When man was in the state of innocence, God was our Lord and Master; now He is our Friend, our Guest, and our Food.

Chapter Ten

Communion lets you approach God with confidence

"Take heart; it is I."

Cf. Matthew 14:27

The purpose of the Eucharist is not only to bring man back to God by destroying the instinctive fear that rules him, but, in addition, to fill his heart with confidence. Strictly speaking, we might be able to bear the presence of God, but who would dare address our Lord unless He first mercifully veiled Himself? He discharges all debts, wipes out all inequalities. Before, on earth, the splendor of the Godhead was so hidden beneath human features that neither sinners nor little children feared to approach Jesus. They saw only His goodness and mercy.

But who will dare speak to our Lord today in the glory and triumph of His Resurrection? He has received the title of Judge of the living and the dead, and, as such, He wishes to be feared and adored. Certainly He is still the good God, the God of mercy; but His state is changed, and if we did not have the Eucharist, we would be unable to speak to Him with simple confidence. Our Lord instituted His Sacrament so that we might love Him, so that He might meet with the same tenderness and affection He received during His mortal life.

On earth, the goodness of our Lord was recognized from His entire manner. His whole person emanated sweetness and attracted souls. Now He is veiled, but the same attributes appear through the cloud that hides Him. This cloud does not hide Him so completely that, when we think of Him, we could ever picture Him otherwise than as gentle and loving. Thus He has imprinted His likeness in souls with the colors of the tenderest love. Looking upon the Sacred Species, we remember at once all that Jesus was and all that He is: love, goodness, mercy, and tenderness. "Behold the Lamb of God!"[39]

Familiarity must manifest itself primarily in sweet confidences and converse. Words are spoken that thrill and irresistibly transport us. The multitude, hearing our Lord, exclaimed, "Never did man speak like this man!"[40] Sinners were touched by the gentleness of His words, and they could not resist His goodness.

For us, the voice of Jesus is heard inwardly. What is this speech, this language of friendship? Doubtless you have heard it many a time. It is naturally sweet — at times severe, but rarely so. It is irresistible. Have you never sat recollected at the feet of Jesus and heard Him say to you when your repentance was sincere, "Come, I forgive you; be not afraid"? And did not happy tears make answer to Him? Oh, the inner voice is more penetrating than material sound! The hearing of the soul is more finely attuned than that of the body. Nothing is truer. In the Holy Trinity is a Word, the type of all words; it is wholly interior and nevertheless real. It is the Word Eternal. Even the simple memory of the words of a father or a mother who has passed on touches our heart and makes the one or the other live again for us. Thus, there are words that are inner, spiritual. But, above all, the word of truth, the word that moves the soul, is interior. The external word by itself has no power to move.

[39] John 1:29.

[40] John 7:46.

Communion lets you approach God

The word of Jesus in the Eucharist is most intimate, penetrating to the very depths of the soul. What brings this poor soul that has neither virtues nor merits, but which knows and frankly confesses as much, to approach our Lord and speak to Him with the freedom and simplicity of a little child toward his mother? What but this same sweetness of intimacy? Would this soul dare speak with such unreserve before witnesses? No, it has heard Jesus saying to it, "Come to me, you who are burdened, and I will refresh you," and it has come. Now, in secret, it speaks freely; it lets itself go with a touching abandon.

This is the sweet, intimate invitation that calls us to Communion; without it, we would never dare to approach the Holy Table. For the grace that prepares for Communion is the grace of confidence, not the grace of examen,[41] nor even the grace of prayer. These are desirable, of course; but to be truly prepared is to have confidence in that "Come, be not afraid; I am the God of your heart." Such a preparation gives much more honor to God than if you were to cast yourself to the earth in despair.

Perhaps you will say to me, "But I am dry and lacking in devotion when I receive Communion. Nothing comes of it." That is because you do not hearken to the intimate words of our Lord, because you do not sit at His feet with the self-forgetfulness of Magdalene, who wept tears of joy even when Jesus spoke not a word to her. Just enter into that secret word of His which is simply the manifestation of His sweetness. One cannot eat and work at the same time. The heavenly Bread you are going to receive is no other than the Word Eternal, the Word of life. You must hear it in peace and repose.

[41] That is, the daily examination of conscience.

Recollection is even more necessary for thanksgiving after Communion than for preparation for it. If you start making one act after another, that is childish. That you should take measures in the course of your thanksgiving to keep up your devotion, in case you are not recollected, is well and good. But wait a little while. You have a Friend within, and simple courtesy demands that you listen to Him. That, alas, is just what you do not want to do!

This is not understanding our Lord's thought aright. You imagine He comes to us to reproach us for our faults. No, such is not the case. A friend does not come to reproach us, and, above all, he does not begin that way. Bear in mind that our Lord never reproaches us in the first moments of Communion. That is the Devil troubling our thoughts in order to prevent us from enjoying the sweet communications of Jesus. He tries to make our Lord out to be a strict Master, a stern Judge, and, in that way, he frightens us. We are almost persuaded to abandon our thanksgiving in order to escape the eye of vengeance. Oh, that is not our Lord's character!

Slothful souls give themselves up at once to thoughts like this: "I am so poor, so sinful." But let your heart once be opened, and a single glance at yourself will be enough to humble you more effectively than all such efforts. Does the rich benefactor, visiting the poor man on his pallet, parade his own riches and nobility upon his entrance, making comparisons between them and the miserable condition of the one he comes to help? No, certainly not; it would be better to stay away than to humiliate him so. On the contrary, he encourages him, consoles him, and makes himself as lowly as possible in order to gain his confidence.

So, if you do not enjoy the consolations of Jesus when He comes to visit you, it is because you do not take time to do so. Be free; open your heart. Jesus cannot do everything alone. The Holy Scripture tells us that the Lord called Samuel in the middle of the night to make a revelation to him, but Samuel did not recognize His voice, never having heard it before. Twice he went to sleep again, until the high priest gave him the secret of receiving divine communications, telling him he must pray God to speak to him and himself be ready to listen. And the Lord called again: "Samuel, Samuel." And Samuel made answer: "Speak, Lord, for Thy servant heareth."[42] Then the Lord revealed to him the secrets of the future.

That is what we must do. Our Lord comes to us, but we must enter into a communion with Him corresponding with the grace of the moment, which is the grace of intimate friendship. Yes, beyond doubt, all the divine attributes belong to our Lord. But as the Eucharist is the highest degree, the full expression of the love of God, so His character in Communion is sweetness and goodness — goodness not like the goodness of Heaven, not even like the goodness He showed during His life on earth, but goodness that corresponds to His sacramental state, that is, a confidential and heart-to-heart intimacy.

That is the true way to enter into communion with our Lord. How do you venture to come to Communion if not because you have heard a sweet voice calling you — you especially — with a goodness that absorbs your attention and keeps you from thinking of anything else: "Come!" Then, hardly is our Lord within your breast when you cry out, carried

[42] 1 Kings 3:4-10 (RSV = 1 Sam. 3:4-10).

away with wonder, "Lord, how good Thou art!" And that is the universal feeling of all communicants; it is instinctive — proof that the goodness and sweetness of the Eucharist are the two divine means by which God reunites fallen man to Himself, by which He attaches him to Himself with the bonds of friendship and intimate confidence.

Chapter Eleven

Communion drives sadness from your soul

"I was kind and beloved in my power.
Behold, I am perishing of deep
grief in a strange land."

1 Maccabees 6:11, 13 (RSV)

We are tormented by a great sadness. It is fixed in the depths of our heart and will not be dislodged therefrom. There is no joy for us on the face of the earth that is not fleeting and that does not end in tears; there is none and can be none. This sorrow comes to us as an integral part of our heritage from Adam, through whose sin we are exiles from our native land and from our Father's house.

We feel this sadness most deeply when we are quite alone. It even frightens us at times. It is there within us, and whence it comes, we know not. People without faith grow discouraged, fall into despair, and prefer death to such a life. That is a terrible sin and a sign of reprobation.

What remedy, then, shall we Christians employ against this innate sadness? The practice of virtue and striving for Christian perfection? These are not enough. Trials and temptations will sometimes even enable this sadness to overcome us. And when it holds sway in our heart, we can say nothing and do nothing. We are overwhelmed by it; our strength is outdone.

Even our Lord, in the Garden of Gethsemane, came near dying of sadness. And during the thirty-three years of His life, He felt its force. Gentle and good though He was, He was sorrowful; for He had taken our infirmities upon Himself. See how our Lord wept![43] The Gospel remarks it, but does not mention that He ever laughed.

The saints, like their Master, passed their lives in sadness — a sadness, however, that they based on supernatural motives: their exiled state, the evil they saw around them, their inability to give to God the glory they would have liked to have given Him.

A remedy, therefore, is necessary for this general evil. And this remedy consists in not remaining shut up in oneself or by oneself. Our sorrow must have an outlet, lest it carry us away like a torrent. Beware, however, of seeking human consolation, as some do, confiding in a friend or a director. That will not meet your need; it will avail nothing, especially if God has sent an increase of sadness to test you. On the contrary, seeing that sympathy and fatherly advice have not chased away the clouds of gloom and restored their joy, people fall back into an even greater darkness. Then Satan takes advantage of their state to lead them to distrust God. And one sees souls, even the purest and holiest, flee terror-stricken from God and from His voice, as Adam did in Paradise.

Prayer itself can, to be sure, somewhat relieve our sadness, but cannot give joy that is unalloyed or of long duration. Although our Lord prayed for hours in Gethsemane, yet His sorrow did not leave Him; He only received the strength to bear it. Likewise a good confession gives us a little peace, but the thought of having offended so good a God very quickly casts us down again.

Then where is the true remedy?

[43] Cf. John 11:35.

Communion drives sadness from your soul

The absolute remedy, the ever-new and ever-effective remedy that sadness cannot withstand, is Communion. Our Lord has made Himself the Eucharist and enters into us to give direct combat to our sadness. And I state as a principle that no soul that truly desires and hungers to receive Jesus will remain sorrowful in Communion. Afterward, sadness may return, because it is inherent in our exiled state. And the more speedily we fall back on ourselves and cease to dwell in the thought of our Lord's goodness, the more quickly it will return, but never at the moment our Lord enters into us.

I appeal also to your personal experience: whenever you were sorrowful before Communion in spite of a good confession, did you not feel joy reborn again in your heart as soon as our Lord made His entrance there? Was not Zacchaeus, the publican, overcome with joy at receiving Jesus? Yet he had great reason to be sad on account of the plundering of which people openly accused him.

The two disciples of Emmaus were sorrowful along the way, even though our Lord accompanied them, spoke to them, and taught them. But after the breaking of the bread, they were filled with joy; their hearts overflowed with gladness, and notwithstanding that it was night, that the way was long, and that they were already fatigued, they hurried back to Jerusalem to make known their happiness and share it with the Apostles.[44]

Now, here is a sinner who has committed every kind of crime. He confesses; his wounds are bound up, and his convalescence begins. He feels a constant sadness; his conversion has made him more sensitive, and he bewails now what before

[44] Luke 24:13-35.

he did not even feel: the sorrow he has caused to God. The more sincere and intelligent his conversion is, the deeper is his sorrow. "I have sinned so greatly against God, who is so good!" he says to himself. If he is left to himself, sorrow will overwhelm him, and the Devil will drive him to despair. But have him go to Communion; let him but feel God's goodness within him, and joy and peace will spread through his soul. "What!" he will say. "I have received the Bread of angels! Am I not, then, the friend of God?" His past sins trouble him no more in this moment. Has not our Lord Himself told him that he is forgiven? And how can he doubt His word?

The joy that Communion gives is the best proof of God's presence in the Eucharist! Our Lord manifests Himself by making Himself felt. "He that loveth me shall be loved of my Father. And I will love him and will manifest myself to him."[45] Our Lord manifests Himself by the joy that always accompanies Him.

Note, for your guidance, that there are two kinds of joy. The one comes from the good we have done, from the practice of virtue. It is the joy of success, the joy of harvest and of victory. Although it is good, seek it not. Since it depends on you, it has not so very firm a foundation, and you might draw too great satisfaction from it.

But the other, the joy of Communion, comes, we are obliged to admit, not from ourselves but only from Jesus, and has no relation to our works. Let us accept that joy without fear when our Lord bestows it upon us; let us find sweet rest therein, for it comes wholly from Him.

[45] John 14:21.

Communion drives sadness from your soul

The child has no virtue, no merit. Yet he rejoices, happy to be at his mother's side. In like manner, let our own joy spring solely from the presence of our Lord. Do not ask yourself whether the joy you feel has been merited in any degree by your works; simply be glad in the possession of Jesus and remain at His feet, enjoying your happiness and rejoicing in His goodness.

Many fear to let the thought of God's goodness occupy them too much, because it demands that one give in return one's entire self without counting the cost. Better, they think, to fulfill the law and have no further obligation. What niggardly calculation from souls to whom our Lord gives Himself so generously!

Let us, instead, enjoy without fear the goodness of God; let us eagerly receive the happiness that is offered us and be ready to give with generosity to our Lord whatever He is pleased to ask of us in return.

Chapter Twelve

Christ speaks to your heart

"And they shall all be taught of God."

John 6:45

In accordance with the honor that kingly majesty owes to itself, the education of a prince is placed in the care of some very learned, noble, and distinguished man. When the young prince is grown, the king himself will teach him the art of ruling men. He alone may teach him this art, because he alone practices it.

We Christians are all princes of Jesus Christ; we are of the blood royal. Our Lord confides the formation of our youth to His ministers, who tell us of God, explaining His nature and His attributes. They show Him to us, promise Him to us, but they cannot make us feel Him or comprehend His goodness. So Jesus Christ Himself comes on the day of our First Communion to make us feel the hidden and inmost meaning of all the instructions we have received. What words and books were powerless to accomplish, Jesus Himself comes to do: to reveal Himself to the soul. This is assuredly the triumph of the Eucharist — that it molds the spiritual man, forms Jesus Christ within us. Our interior education will always be incomplete, unless it is the work of our Lord Himself.

So Jesus comes to us to teach us all truth. One who does not go to Communion has only a theoretical knowledge. He knows only terms for the most part, being ignorant of the things for which they stand. Jesus has not manifested Himself to him. Such a person may know the definition, the rule of a virtue, and the progressive stages necessary in its development; he does not know our Lord Himself. He is like the blind man of the Gospel who, before he knew our Lord, called Him a great prophet, a friend of God. But when Jesus Christ had revealed Himself to him, he saw God, fell at His feet, and adored Him.[46]

The soul, likewise, that before Communion has had only an idea and knowledge of our Lord gained from books, sees and recognizes Him with rapture at the Holy Table. Our Lord is not truly made known to us except through Himself. We then learn the truth from living and substantial Truth. Enravished, we cry out, "My Lord and my God!"[47] As the sun manifests itself by its own light, so Jesus Christ manifests Himself not by the light of reason, but by His own light.

This intimate revelation impels the spirit to seek the hidden meaning of the mysteries, to sound the depths of the love and the goodness of God in His works. This knowledge is not like ordinary science, dry and sterile; it is sweet and full of affection. One knows and one feels at the same time. It is a knowledge that impels to love, inflames, and urges to action. Through it, we enter into the heart of the mysteries; our adoration after Communion, moved by the grace of Communion, is not content to remain on the surface but sees, searches into, and contemplates the divine plan: "It searcheth the deep things of God."[48] We go from clarity to clarity, as in Heaven.

The Savior appears to us under an aspect ever new. Although the subject of our meditation is always Jesus living

[46] Cf. John 9:1-38.

[47] John 20:28.

[48] 1 Cor. 2:10.

within us, our meditation is never the same. There are abysses of love in Jesus that must be penetrated with a loving and active faith. Oh, if we dared to search the depths of our Lord, how we would love Him! But in our apathy, our indolence, we are content with the gifts already received and with a superficial understanding. Our sloth fears lest it be roused to love, for the more this knowledge of the heart increases, the more we are forced to love.

The education given us by Communion, by Jesus in us, trains for love, calls forth frequent acts of love, and thereby leads us to all virtues. Jesus, by the intimate and striking manifestation of His love for us, teaches us to love Him. He convinces us that He gives us all He has, all He is; by the very excess of His love for us, He forces us to love Him. As a mother awakens love for her in the heart of her child simply by loving him, so our Lord acts toward us.

It is impossible for anyone to bestow upon us a love for Jesus Christ or infuse it into our hearts. People may exhort us to love Him, but it is beyond human power to teach us how to love; we learn love by feeling it. This education of the heart belongs to our Lord alone, for He desires Himself alone to be its goal. He begins by giving to the communicant the sentiment of love, then the motive of love, and finally the impelling desire for the heroism of love. But this is learned only in Communion. "Except you eat the Flesh of the Son of Man and drink His Blood, you shall not have life in you."[49]

What life is meant but the life of love — that powerful life which has its source only in Jesus Himself?

[49] John 6:54 (RSV = John 6:53).

Is it not in the act of Communion that we feel ourselves most greatly loved by Jesus? True, we weep with joy after our sins are forgiven, but the remembrance of them keeps us from being completely happy. Only in Communion is happiness to be found in its fullness. There only do we see and weigh all the sacrifices of Jesus Christ. There, overcome by so much love, we end by crying out from the depths of our heart, "My God, my God, how canst Thou love me so much?"

And we rise from the Holy Table in a glow of love: "Like lions with a breath of fire."[50] We feel what measureless ingratitude it would be to give nothing in return for such goodness. At first, we are overwhelmed by our nothingness; then, conscious that we are unable of ourselves to do anything, but strong in Him who dwells within us, we go from virtue to virtue. Love so experienced always calls forth a corresponding devotion.

Love shows us what we have to do. It takes us out of ourselves, makes us emulate the virtues of our Lord, and withdraws us from this world into Him. Our education thus begun goes fast and far. The reason so many Christians get no farther than the threshold of virtue is that they will not break the chains that hold them back and will not give themselves up confidently to our Lord's guidance. They feel that if they go to Communion, they will be unable to resist the love of Jesus and be forced to give themselves in return. So they content themselves with books, with words, and do not dare turn to the Master Himself.

Oh, my brothers, I pray you to take Jesus Christ Himself for your Teacher! Receive Him within you, and let Him direct all

[50] St. John Chrysostom, Homily 61 to the people of Antioch.

your actions. Take care not to be satisfied with the Gospel alone and with Christian traditions. Do not be content to meditate on mysteries long past. Jesus is here, living. He contains within Himself all the mysteries; all are alive in Him, and their grace has its source in Him. So give yourselves to Jesus Christ! Let Him dwell in you, and you will bear much fruit, according to the promise He Himself makes you: "He that abideth in me, and I in him, the same beareth much fruit."[51]

[51] John 15:5.

Chapter Thirteen

Christ gives Himself to you in particular

"My Beloved to me, and I to Him."

Canticles 2:16
(RSV = Song of Solomon 2:16)

To possess Jesus and be possessed by Him: that is love in its highest manifestation; that is the life of union between the soul and Jesus, which is nourished reciprocally by the gift of each one to the other. The Beloved in the Blessed Sacrament belongs wholly to me by the entire, perfect, personal, and perpetual gift of Himself. I must belong to Him in the same manner.

"My Beloved to me." In all the other mysteries, by all His graces, Jesus gives us something: His grace, His merits, His example. In Holy Communion, He gives Himself entire. He gives Himself in His two natures together with the graces and merits of all the states through which He has passed.

What a gift! "He gives all who keeps nothing for Himself." Is not this the Eucharistic gift? Whence could the thought have come to our Lord to give Himself thus but from His Heart, burning with a boundless love for man?

O Heart of Jesus,
infinitely generous Heart,
be Thou praised and blessed forever!

Jesus, who loves each one of us in particular, gives Himself to each one. Love that is general little moves us. But we cannot resist a love that is shown to us personally. That God loved the world is very beautiful; but that He loves me, myself, tells me so, and, to convince me, gives Himself to me — that is the triumph of His love. For Jesus comes for me; I might say He comes for me alone. I am the object of this mystery of infinite power and love that is being enacted on the holy altar, for it aims at me and is perfected in me.

O love, what shall I give in return? That I, poor creature that I am, should occupy thus the thought of Jesus Christ! That I should be the goal of His love!

Oh, live and reign in me, my God!
I desire not that Thou should
have loved me in vain!

This magnificent gift is not subject to recall, but is ours forever. Happiness that must someday come to an end is shadowed always by fear or sorrow. Heaven, if it were not everlasting, would no longer be Heaven. Its happiness would no more be unalloyed. But the Eucharist is a perpetual gift that will last as long as the love that inspired it. I have a definite promise of that. Whatever vicissitudes occur, Jesus will close the procession of the centuries and be with His Church until the end of the world.

What happiness to have Jesus in my company, in my possession and ownership! No one can take Him from me. I find Him everywhere; like the sun, He gives light and life to all. Companion in my exile, Bread of my pilgrimage, He will go with me and sustain me until I reach the haven of salvation. Oh, sweet exile! Happy journey made with Jesus to accompany me!

"And I to Him!" I must belong to Jesus Christ as He belongs to me; otherwise there would be no true fellowship. As Jesus thinks and labors for me alone, so I must live only for Him. He must be the inspiration of my thoughts, the goal of my knowledge, or else my mind would not belong to Him. He must be God of my heart, the law and center of its affections. Every love, every affection that is not from Him, and by Him, and in Him, that has not Him for its goal, prevents the perfect union of my heart with His. I do not give Him my heart if I keep back any part of it.

Jesus must be the supreme guide of my will and my desires. What He wills, I also will, and what He desires, that only will I desire. His thought must govern all the motions of my body, impose upon my senses modesty and respect for His presence. This is the first commandment in operation: "Thou shalt love the Lord thy God with thy whole heart, and with thy whole soul, and with all thy strength."[52]

Love is one in its affection, universal in its operation; it rules everything by a single principle, applying it to all duties, however varied and numerous they may be.

Do I belong wholly to Jesus, as I should in obedience to justice, to love especially, and to the promise I made, the promise which Jesus accepted and confirmed by His graces and favors?

Jesus gives me His entire person; therefore I owe to Him my entire self, my person, my individuality, my *ego*. In order to make this gift, I have to renounce all self-seeking, whatever form it may take. I must renounce all esteem of myself that, based on my qualities, my talents, or the services I may have been able to render, is directed specially and finally toward me, instead of passing onward to God. Every affection that has

[52] Luke 10:27.

me as its only object I must renounce likewise, and that with the delicacy of feeling of a wife who desires neither to attract the love nor to accept the attentions of any but her husband. I must seek the affection of others only in order to lead them to Jesus, who alone is worthy of attracting the heart's deepest yearning.

To give up my personality is to renounce myself in my pleasures, offering them to Jesus; it is to keep for Him, and for Him alone, the secret of my sorrows. Then only will He live within me when, in place of me, He Himself shall receive the esteem and affection given me by others; otherwise I myself still live, and not Jesus alone in me.

Finally, since the gift Jesus gives to me in the Holy Eucharist is perpetual, I must, in return, belong to Him forever. The reasons for continuing to love Him are the selfsame reasons that caused me to begin. They increase constantly, becoming each day more pressing as, each day, Jesus renews for me His miracles of love.

I must belong to Him, therefore, with equal abandon in every vocation, in every interior state, in joy and in tears, in fervor and in aridity, in peace and in temptation, in health and in pain. As Jesus gives Himself to me in all these states, so I also must give myself in return.

I must be His, again, in every employment. The different labors to which Providence appoints me are only exterior appearances, different forms of life. Jesus gives Himself in all of them, demanding a like gift of myself in all.

Who shall separate me from the love of Jesus, who is in me, who lives in me, who urges me and impels me to love Him? Neither tribulation, nor distress, nor famine, nor nakedness, nor danger, nor persecution, nor the sword! All these things we shall overcome for love of Him who first so much loved us!"[53]

But there are three ways in which we may belong to Jesus. First, there is the love that follows the law, that fulfills its duty and is content with that. We must all have this love; it is the love of the conscience, which admonishes us not to offend God. This love has different degrees and may attain to great perfection.

When we think of what God might, with justice, demand of us as our Creator, our Redeemer, and our Sanctifier, we are astonished that He should condescend to reward with Heaven all whose love is this mere faithfulness to duty. Yet such is His measureless goodness. And even so, sad to relate, there are many who refuse Heaven even on these terms!

Then there is the love of self-devotion. This is the love of so many holy souls who, living in the world, practice the virtues of the cloister: faithful virgins, true lilies among thorns; devoted wives, governing their families according to the plan of God and bringing up their children solely for His glory; widows consecrated to His service in prayer and works of mercy. Of this kind, also, is the love practiced by the religious in monasteries. It is a great, free, and tender love; it impels the soul to place itself at the disposition of the divine good pleasure. It is a love that gives great glory to God; it is the apostolate of His goodness.

But supreme over all is the heart's royal love. This is the love of the Christian who gives to God not only his faith, his piety, and his liberty, but likewise every pleasure of his life. Yes,

[53] Cf. Rom. 8:35, 37.

he gives even the pleasure that belongs legitimately to the practice of piety, his joy in the Christian life, in his good works, in prayer, and in Communion.

Offer one's spiritual joys and pleasures to God in sacrifice to His will? Renounce one's intimate and personal pleasures? Suffer lovingly, silently, for Jesus, making Him one's sole Confidant and Consoler and Protector? But who does this or even thinks of it?

Is it even possible? Yes, to genuine love it is possible. Therein lies the true delicacy of love, its real power — even, I shall say, its ineffable happiness. "I exceedingly abound with joy in all our tribulation,"[54] cried that great lover of Jesus, St. Paul.

May we also be able to say, "Jesus is sufficient for me. I am faithful to Him. His love is my whole life."

[54] 2 Cor. 7:4.

Chapter Fourteen

Communion lets you surrender yourself to Christ

"As Thou, Father, in me, and I in Thee;
that they also may be one in us."

John 17:21

God's union with us crowns the divine work of rehabilitation accomplished by Communion. *Communion:* the very name is significant! It is not a moral union, a union of sentiment or of friendship. No, it is a union of substances, approaching more nearly than any other, except the divine maternity, to the hypostatic union.[55]

By the Incarnation, human nature was united to the divine nature in unity of person, so that one who saw the body of our Lord saw God. Now Jesus Christ, God and Man, enters into us and enacts a mystery similar to the one wrought in Mary's womb. St. Augustine, speaking of the dignity of the priest, exclaimed, "O awesome dignity of the priests, in whose hands, as in the womb of the Virgin, the Son of God becomes incarnate!"[56] By the hands of the priest, the Eucharist passes into our bodies and, uniting with us, prolongs, extends, the Incarnation to each of us separately. In becoming incarnate in the Virgin Mary, the Word had in view this incarnation in each one of us, this Communion with the individual soul; it was one of the ends for which He came into the world. Communion is

[55] That is, the substantial union of the divine and human natures in the person of Christ.

[56] St. Augustine (354-430; Bishop of Hippo), *On the Psalms*.

the perfect development, the full unfoldment of the Incarnation, as it is likewise the completion of the sublime Sacrifice of Calvary, renewed each day in the Mass. It is in order to be united with His priest and the faithful that Jesus Christ descends to the altar at the Consecration; without Communion, the Sacrifice would be incomplete.

Thus the body of Jesus Christ is united with our body, His soul with our soul, and His divinity hovers over both. Our body is encased, so to speak, in the body of our Lord. As the greater and nobler of the two, His body dominates and envelops us. We are clothed therein; it is the body of our body; its blood flows in our veins; we are fused into it in an ineffable union.

How wonderful is this incorporation of a glorious, resurrected body with our miserable nature! And this sight is enjoyed by God and His angels; our earthly eyes do not see it. It is a heavenly spectacle.

When two lumps of wax are melted together by the action of fire, they coalesce and are one, yet the elements of both are still present and could be separated. In Communion, the union is the same. We lose the corporal presence of Christ when the Species are consumed; but, if sin does not drive our Lord away, our body continues to participate in the virtues of the body of Jesus, receiving its force, grace, integrity, and morals. Our body lives on our Lord's vital energy; it becomes spiritualized.

Do you not feel after Communion that your passions are weakened, that peace reigns in your members? Just as ice reduces fevers, so Jesus heals the fever of our concupiscence by the purity of His virginal body.

St. Cyril says that we become through Communion "blood-kindred of Jesus Christ."[57] The Blood of Jesus Christ flows in our veins. We are changed into Him. "I will not be changed into you, nor will you change me into you as you do the food of your flesh; but you will be changed into me."[58] "We are merged with Jesus," said St. Chrysostom.[59] So let us give our body to be recast in this divine mold and develop therein unto eternal glory.

But the soul? Jesus Christ comes straight to our soul and says, "I will espouse you to me forever."[60] The soul is above all else the goal for which Jesus aims in us. Although the body is first honored, it is but the antechamber; our Lord only passes that way. The soul receives Him and shares in His divine life, being as if lost in Him. Jesus begins by causing it to be penetrated with the feeling of His goodness, not yet asking anything of it in return. This happiness is immediate if the soul is deeply absorbed in the Lord's goodness and thinks only of that. Jesus is like the morning sun, at whose rising everything awakens and opens into bloom.

It is our Lord's desire to communicate Himself to us as abundantly as possible. But each one receives Him according to his capacity and preparation. To the soul that is well prepared, He gives a strength of life, a generous resolution that causes it to vow eternal fidelity to its Spouse. Henceforth it studies His wishes, tries to find ways of pleasing Him. It

[57] St. Cyril (c. 315-386; Bishop of Jerusalem), *Catecheses*.

[58] St. Augustine, *Confessions*, Bk. 7, ch. 10.

[59] St. John Chrysostom, Homily 60.

[60] Osee 2:19 (RSV = Hos. 2:19).

receives from our Lord that delicate sense by which He discerns the things that are to His Father's glory, the faculty of judging everything from the divine viewpoint. A soul that lacks this delicate perception seeks itself in all things and, even in receiving Communion, thinks only of the sweetness it may draw from our Lord's presence. Delicacy of feeling is the flower of love.

To a soul so finely attuned, Jesus Christ gives, moreover, the grace of self-forgetfulness and entire self-surrender. A soul that receives Communion must come to the point of loving our Lord for Himself, must be able to give itself without asking what it will receive in return. He loves little who demands a recompense for everything he does. To live by Jesus for oneself is well and good, but to live by Him and for Him is better. See what Jesus asked of St. Peter: "Lovest thou me more than these?" "Yea, Lord, Thou knowest that I love Thee." But Jesus repeated His question a second and a third time. Then St. Peter was grieved.[61] He wept, and his tears were an avowal of his deep desire to love more than all the others. Our Lord was well content then and gave to St. Peter the charge of feeding His lambs and His sheep. He laid upon Him the heaviest burden man ever bore and promised no reward.

Our Lord wants us to forget about ourselves. He requires those who truly love Him to lose themselves utterly, to leave entirely to Him without calculation all their interests of soul and body for time and for eternity. Being distrustful, asking wages, keeping something back — all this is usually a sign of laziness. It costs little to tell God we love Him when He is

[61] John 21:15-17.

showering favors upon us; it is in the midst of the tempest that we must cry out to Him like Job: "Although He should kill me, I will trust Him!"[62] In this case, we give our very self; in the other, we give merely from our surplus.

Our Lord is certainly not seeking His own interests in the love He shows us. He has no need of us; He loves us only for our own good, only to make us happy. He asks everything from us, and if we wish really to love Him as He loves us, we will not stop to think so much of what we shall receive in return. Does this mean we shall receive no reward, be given nothing in exchange for this entire gift of ourselves? Certainly not! Our Lord asks everything from us, so that He may give us even more in return, like the mother who, to test her child's affection, demands his little toys and then gives them back with others still finer, happy to see that her child loves her more than anything else.

Oh, give everything to our Lord, you souls who live by Communion! Give your works and your merits, your heart with all its inclinations — even those that are most proper and most lawful! It is a hard struggle, in which the poor human heart suffers agony; but when one thinks of whom one gives to, oh, how quickly the decision is made!

Communion is likewise the means by which our Lord unites us with His Father. If the heavenly Father gave us our reward solely on our personal merits, as His creatures, we could expect no more than a natural happiness. But our Lord has shared our human nature, and, by Communion, He renews and strengthens that relationship. He proves thereby to His Father how

[62] Job 13:15.

much He loves us, how greatly He desires us to be united to Him, and the Father is obliged to crown us together with His Son. He cannot separate Head and Heart from the other members. Thus Communion gives us such easy access to Heaven that one might almost say that Jesus Christ brings us into glory by stratagem.

But the Eucharist is most sublime in this, that Jesus lived His earthly life only for the glory of His Father. Having ascended into Heaven, He did not wish His Father to cease receiving the homage of His acts as God and Man. So, continuing and multiplying Himself in His good communicants, He presents them to His Father, saying, "I have entered into my glory at Thy right hand; but I become incarnate again in all these Christians, that through them and in them I may honor Thee anew. I wish to make them and myself one in Thy glory."

Oh, can one fail to wonder at the way our happiness, by our Lord's wisdom, is bound up with the glory of His Father? Who can comprehend the Son's marvelous love for His Father and for us? What divine intelligence is exercised in order to render us deserving of a richer recompense, to make us participants in glory!

So let Communion be the center of our life, of our actions. Live in order to receive Communion, and receive Communion in order to live a holy life and give glory to God within you. He will one day give you glory beyond telling in the blissful eternity that is His.

Chapter Fifteen

Prayer is essential to fruitful Communion

"Christ your life."

Cf. Colossians 3:4

We must live on the Eucharist. The Eucharist is love, nothing but love; therefore, we must perfect this love within us, continually renewing its fire, so that we ourselves may be enkindled by it. Love must be made strong in our hearts before we may expect to make it manifest in good works. Since we receive Incarnate Love so often, our whole life should be simply the development and unfoldment of this love. But if we do not take pains to bring love to perfection in our hearts, we shall never make any progress. Let us be true disciples of Jesus Christ and live by love. The Holy Spirit has breathed the spirit of love into our hearts; let us love, then, bounteously, generously, and royally!

God infinitely diversifies His gifts. Yet there are certain attractions of grace that are found over and over again — in souls He wishes to sanctify in one and the same way. This is the source of the religious orders, in which those gather together whom God has called by identical graces. You who seek your sanctification in the Holy Eucharist must live the completely inward and hidden life that Jesus lives in the Blessed Sacrament. The Eucharist is the fruit of the love of Jesus Christ, and the heart is the seat of love. In order to make us realize this truth, our Lord does not let us see Him but remains in the Holy Eucharist, imperceptible to the senses; we neither perceive His Body nor taste His Blood. He wants us to go on and find His love in the depths of His Heart.

In the Most Blessed Sacrament, Jesus practices the virtues of His earthly life, but in a wholly invisible and interior way. Ever contemplating the glory of His Father, He lives in prayer, continually making intercession for us. He wants us to see that prayer is the secret of the interior life; that we must tend the roots of the tree if we wish to harvest good fruit; that the external life so esteemed by the world is only a sterile flower without the aliment of charity that will make it fruitful. Give your life to contemplation of Jesus, therefore, if you wish to be successful in your labors.

The Apostles, complaining that they had not enough time for prayer, chose deacons to relieve them of the burden of the outward ministry.[63] Jesus Christ, during His life on earth, escaped from the crowd, retired apart, and hid Himself in order to enter into prayer and contemplation.[64] So how could we expect to live a wholly external life? Are our graces more abundant and our forces for good greater than those of the Apostles? And is our Lord's example not meant for us? Piety, in order to repair its losses and renew its life, must have recourse to prayer and to recollection in Jesus Christ, its center; otherwise, it will wither away and die.

Only in prayer do the fruits of virtue ripen; only in prayer are they harvested. By prayer, a soul may save the world, because it is united with Jesus Christ, who prays within His tabernacle.

[63] Acts 6:2-4.

[64] Cf. Matt. 14:23.

All virtues come from God, and it is from the Eucharist, above all, that Jesus causes them to stream into our souls in floods of grace by the examples He gives us of them there. But we must see these examples, contemplate them, study them, let them fill our minds. Where shall we obtain a greater love of humility than before the Sacred Host? Where shall we find more beautiful examples of silence, patience, and meekness?

In the Most Holy Sacrament, our Lord no longer practices outwardly the sublime virtues of His mortal life. His wisdom no longer gives utterance to divine maxims; no vestige appears of His power and His glory. To be poor, little, simple — that is His eucharistic life. Poverty of spirit, mildness, and patience are what He shows us; and what tender consideration that is on His part!

Occasions demanding heroic virtues are rare in life, and we have hardly the courage to take advantage of them. Shall we despair, then, and abandon the spiritual life under pretext of being unable to do anything for God? Jesus makes His eucharistic life a remedy against this temptation, teaching us that sanctity finds its exercise above all in little things. His self-effacement and His absence of outward activity teach us that the inward life, consisting wholly of the acts of our heart, the outpourings of our love, the union of our intentions with His, is the most perfect of all. Oh, God loves very specially the humble, the little ones who stay at His feet, under the heavenly influence of His Heart!

Nor does the life of prayer exclude zeal for the salvation of souls. One who leads the interior life is able, even while working, to preserve his state of recollection; he is not the less active in the external world, like Jesus who, invisible though He is, makes Himself felt. The sinner who prays to Him feels the sweetness of His Heart. Between the soul and Jesus, there is set in motion an unseen current; an inaudible colloquy is carried on. No one discerns this activity of our Lord in the depths of the soul, yet how real it is! Oh, let us strive to make our zeal like that of Jesus, completely hidden, wholly spiritual!

Never think the time you pass in front of the tabernacle is time taken from good works; not until the grain is covered by the furrow does its fecundity appear. Intimacy with the Holy Eucharist is the seed of virtue.

There are plenty of souls nowadays who are given to zealous undertakings. They are greatly praised — too much sometimes. Pray that their inner heart may accord with their outer zeal and that they may give to their soul the sustenance of prayer.

Now, in order that your virtues may please and attract your neighbor, clothe them with the sweetness of Jesus Christ. Nothing is more lovable than simplicity and lack of pretension. Hidden and silent virtue is blessed by all. Patience that comes without effort from the heart, an entirely simple and unfeigned charity — these are the fruits of the hidden life that are developed by the reception of Jesus and by the contemplation of the example offered by His eucharistic life.

Chapter Sixteen

Union with Christ sanctifies your actions

"He that eateth me, the same also shall live by me."

John 6:58
(RSV = John 6:57)

By Communion, Jesus comes to take possession of us and make us His. To enter into His plan, we must abandon to Him all rights over and all ownership in ourselves; we must leave to Him the direction and initiative of all our acts; we must do nothing by ourselves nor for ourselves, but everything by and for Him.

By this union, there takes place within us a new incarnation of the Word, who then continues in us for the glory of God what He did in the human nature of Jesus.

I command the faculties of my soul; my members obey me; it is I, the complete man, who act, who call forth action, and it is I who am responsible for all the movements as well as for all the actions of my being. My powers serve me blindly; the principle that causes them to act is alone responsible for what they do, because they work only by it and for it, and not for themselves.

This being so, it follows that in our Lord, who had two natures but only one Person, that of the Word, these two natures acted at the behest of the Word, and that the least of our Lord's human acts was at the same time a divine act. It was an action of the Word, who alone could inspire it and give it value — an infinite value which it received because it had for its end a divine Person. It also follows therefrom that the human nature of our Lord could not originate anything, that it had no self-interest, and that it acted not for itself but solely as the servant of the Word, who alone was the moving force of all its acts. The Word willed in both His divine and His human nature and acted through each.

It must be the same with us. Or, at least, we must make every effort to approach this divine ideal by which man acts only as a passive instrument moved and guided by a divine force, the Spirit of Jesus Christ, toward the one goal God can set for His activity — that is, Himself and His own glory. We must therefore be dead to every desire and interest of self and have in view only the desires and interests of Jesus within us. He is there only to live again for the glory of His Father. He gives Himself in Holy Communion in order to foster this ineffable union and make it closer.

When the divine Word says in the Gospel, "As the living Father hath sent me, and I live by the Father; so he that eateth me, the same also shall live by me," He seems to say, "In sending me into the world through the Incarnation to be the divine personality of a nature that would have no person of its own, the Father destroyed in this nature every root of self-seeking, in order that it should live for Him alone; likewise, through Communion, I unite myself to you to live in you and cause you to live only for me. In you I shall will and desire, putting myself in place of you; your faculties shall be my faculties; by your heart and mind and senses, I shall live and act; you will possess in me a divine personality, which will give to your actions a superhuman dignity, a divine merit, and make them worthy of God and deserving of beatitude, the intuitive Vision of God. What I am by nature, you will be by grace: sons of God, rightful heirs of His kingdom, His riches and glory."

When our Lord, through His Spirit, lives in us, we are His members, we are Himself. Our actions are acceptable to the Heavenly Father. Seeing them, He sees His divine Son's own actions and is well pleased with them. The Father, inseparably united to His Word, also lives and reigns in us. And this divine life, this divine reign, paralyzes and destroys the rule of Satan. Creatures now render to God the glory and honor He rightly expects from them.

Thus our Lord's primary object in desiring us to be united to Him supernaturally by the life of perfect charity is to give glory to His Father in His members. That is why St. Paul so often calls us "members of the Body of Jesus Christ."[65] That is why our Lord at the Last Supper repeats over and over the words "Abide with me."[66] They imply the entire gift of self, for when one no longer lives in oneself, one labors for Him with whom one lives and is wholly at His disposition.

Our Lord also desires this union from love of us, that He may ennoble us through Himself and share with us one day His celestial glory with all that constitutes it: power, beauty, and perfect happiness. And as our Lord can communicate His glory to us only insofar as we become His members, and as His members are holy, He therefore desires to sanctify us in order to unite us to Him and give us participation in His glorious life.

Even here on earth, our actions become our Lord's actions and derive their value more or less from our Lord's according

[65] Cf. Rom. 12:5; 1 Cor. 12:27.

[66] Cf. John 15:4, 5, 7.

to the closeness of their union with His. And this union means conformity with the morals, the virtues, and the Spirit of Jesus within us. Hence these beautiful words: "The Christian is another Christ. And I live, now not I, but Christ liveth in me."[67] "Yet not I, but the grace of God with me."[68]

This union is the fruit of the love of Jesus Christ; it is the goal of the divine plan in its entirety in the natural and supernatural order. All the institutions of Providence tend to bring about and consummate this union of the Christian with Jesus Christ, tend to foster and perfect it; for in it is comprised the entire glory of God in His creature, all the sanctification of souls — in a word, the entire fruit of the Redemption.

The union of Jesus Christ with us will depend upon our union with Him: "Abide in me, and I in you."[69] "He that eateth my Flesh abideth in me, and I in him."[70] So I may be sure that Jesus will abide in me if I will abide in Him. As the wind rushes into the void, water into the depths, so the Spirit of Jesus at once fills the empty place prepared by the soul.

In this union with our Lord consists man's dignity. I do not become part of the Divinity, something to be adored; yet I become something consecrated, holy. My nature is still nothing in the eyes of God and, of itself, may fall back into the abyss. But God, by His grace, by His presence within me, raises it to union with Him. This union makes me related to our Lord in a degree corresponding with its closeness and the measure of my

[67] Cf. Gal. 2:20.

[68] 1 Cor. 15:10.

[69] John 15:4.

[70] John 6:57 (RSV = John 6:56).

purity and sanctity. In short, relationship with our Lord is simply participation in His sanctity, according to His words: "For whosoever shall do the will of my Father, who is in Heaven, he is my brother, and sister, and mother."[71]

To this union, also, man owes his power. "As the branch cannot bear fruit of itself, unless it abide in the vine, so neither can you, unless you abide in me. Without me you can do nothing."[72] Nothing — that is plainly spoken. Now, as the branch draws its fertility from union with the trunk and the sap, so also spiritual fecundity comes from our union with Jesus Christ, from the union of our thoughts with His thoughts, of our words with His words, of our actions with His actions. The members of the body draw their life from the heart's blood, and the blood is produced by nourishment. But our nourishment is Jesus, the Bread of Life, and only he who eats it has life in him.

This, then, is the source of our strength of holiness: union with our Lord. In the absence of this union, our works are vain, empty, sterile; the withered branch that no longer partakes of the life of the vine can bear no fruit.

Of this union is born the merit of our works. It is a merit of fellowship. Our Lord takes our action and makes it His, causing it to merit an infinite reward, an eternal recompense. This action, as it came from us, was almost nothing, but clothed now as it is with the merits of Jesus, it becomes worthy of God. And the closer our union with Jesus, the greater will be the glory of our holy works.

[71] Cf. Matt. 12:50.

[72] John 15:4, 5.

Oh, what is the reason for our unhappy neglect of this divine union? How many merits we have lost! How many actions we have rendered sterile by not doing them in union with Jesus Christ! How many graces have borne no fruit! What? With such resources at our command and in so easy a transaction, have we gained so little?

Let us then be united with Jesus Christ our Lord! As His human nature was united to the Person of the Word and was submissive and obedient to His rule, as also the complete Jesus Christ was to His Father, so let us be united to our Lord, submitting ourselves docilely to His will and direction, guided by His thought, following His inspirations, and offering Him all our actions. But in order that this may be, we must be united in a union of life — life received, renewed, and sustained by continual communion with Jesus.

It is with us as with the vine branch, which must be expanded and warmed by the sun in order that the sap may fully penetrate it. In like manner, we must be disposed to receive the divine sap by the sun which draws it and maintains it — that is, by recollection, desire, and prayer, by the constant gift of self, by love sighing without rest for Jesus and at every moment mounting impetuously toward Him. "Come, Lord Jesus!"[73] And what is this sap but the blood of Jesus, which gives to us His divine life, strength, and fertility? This life of union may be expressed, therefore, in two terms: sacramental Communion and a life of recollection.

[73] Apoc. 22:20 (RSV = Rev. 22:20).

Chapter Seventeen

Let Communion nourish your interior life

"I will be as the dew, Israel shall spring as the lily, and his root shall shoot forth as that of Libanus."

Osee 14:6
(RSV = Hos. 14:6)

In the garden of our soul, that paradise of God, we have to cultivate the divine grain, Jesus Christ, sown in us by Holy Communion, that it may spring up and produce the flower of sanctity.

Now, in nature, in growing flowers, the essential thing is to keep them fresh by watering the roots. If the root dries, the plant will die. Fertility depends on moisture. The sun by itself does not make flowers bloom; its heat alone would make them wither, but it makes moisture fertile, active. Therefore, to cultivate the flower of sanctity in your soul, you have to keep the roots fresh and moist, which means simply that you have to live the interior life. Nature gives dew and rain to the earth. The grace of God is the dew of the soul; given in abundance, it is a shower that floods it and makes it fruitful.

The cultivation of your soul consists, therefore, in leading a life of recollection.

Beyond doubt, life in the outer world, however holy and apostolic it may be, always makes us lose a little of our recollection, and if we fail to renew this inner self, we end by losing all grace and all supernatural life.

On the other hand, it would seem that, since virtue is meritorious, its outer practice ought to increase our grace every day instead of decreasing it. That is essentially true; virtue naturally has that tendency. But the store of interior life we draw upon is small and is soon expended in action.

We are told in the Gospel how a woman approached our Lord unperceived and touched the hem of His garment. She was healed, but Jesus said, "I know that virtue is gone out from me."[74] Yet Jesus had not lost this strength; His infinite divine power was undiminished. As the sun darts forth its rays and diffuses its heat without exhausting itself, so God gives without being impoverished.

But with us, it is different. When we give our efforts to works of zeal for our neighbor, we decrease our store of supernatural life. This is not, I repeat, something inherent in virtue itself, but it comes from our weakened and degraded state, our constant tendency to fall, so that we never perform external acts of virtue without losing some part of our interior strength and needing to return to the inner life for rest and recuperation.

It is the simple daily occupations to which we are bound by the obligations of our state or by obedience that use up our spiritual reserves. And unless we frequently renew our intention, they will be fatal to us.

We shall become machines, and machines even less perfect than the steam engine, which gives forth constantly and regularly the power of which it is capable, while we ourselves cannot long keep up the same pace. We shall become a monstrous machine! The world is always with us and, however retired our life may be, finds stealthy entrance into our heart. It is so easy to let self-love enter where the love of God alone ought to dwell!

[74] Luke 8:46.

What I say of outside activities and manual labor is true also of study. Even your study of God, of Holy Scripture, of theology, the highest of all knowledge, will puff you up and make your heart arid if you do not unremittingly cultivate the interior life. Your mind will gain ascendancy over your heart and make it an arid waste unless you diligently refresh its life with aspirations, good intentions, and yearnings toward God. Knowledge is only an aid to piety; but piety sanctifies knowledge.

The higher one rises in dignity of office, the greater the loss to one's inner life and the depletion of one's spiritual forces, because everyone draws upon them. For that reason, one has then to pray more. The saints worked in the daytime and prayed at night. The victorious soldier must return to his encampment to rest, or the flag of victory will drape his bier. The harder you work, the greater your need of retreat.

The world is strangely deceived in this regard. "Look," people say. "What a beautiful life! This person sacrifices himself entirely in the service of others." All very good, but on closer examination, I find certain defects in all this good that make me suspicious of so great a zeal. The leaves on this fine tree, it seems to me, are beginning to turn yellow before their time. There must be some inner blight. You see it dying little by little; it lacks the true sap, the inner life.

We must be as closely united to God inwardly as we are in the performance of good works. Well does the Devil know how to make use of our ignorance or neglect of this principle to send us to perdition. When he sees a zealous and generous soul, he urges it on and makes it so absorbed in work that it is unable to look within. He affords it a thousand opportunities to waste its forces, until it is utterly exhausted. While it is thus taken up with the troubles of others, he undermines its defenses and ends by taking full possession of it.

Oh, how quickly we wither beneath the scorching sun of action when our roots do not lie deep in the fresh ground of the inner life!

"But," you say, "I simply must work. There is so much to do. God's work calls me on every side!" True, but take time to eat and sleep if you do not want to lose your wits.

Yes, there is great danger in devoting oneself too assiduously to outside good works unless, like the prophet, we continually watch over our soul to see whether we still keep in the law and walk in the straight way. It is so easy to let oneself be drawn away to the right or to the left, and it is sometimes so brilliant!

Skirmishers render good service in an army; but they are not the ones who carry off the victory. So you must not always be rushing forward but must often retire within yourself to ask God for strength and to meditate on the best way to use it. Here is a practical rule: if, instead of dominating your position, you are dominated by it, you are lost. What will become of a ship, in spite of all the skill of its pilot, when its rudder has been carried away by the tempest? The rudder that guides you and moves you is recollection. Do everything in your power to preserve it, or you will go adrift.

So never say again, "Oh, what a holy soul! See how zealous this person is!" but, "Does he live the interior life?" If so, you may expect everything good from him; if not, he will come to nothing holy or great in the eyes of God.

Therefore, be master of your exterior life; if it masters you, it will hurry you on to destruction. If your occupations leave you opportunity to contemplate our Lord interiorly, you are on the right road; continue on it. If, in the midst of action, your thoughts turn to God; if you know how to prevent dryness and desolation of heart; if your exterior labors always leave you tired and weary, yet conscious of a deep inner peace, oh, then, that is excellent! You are free and, beneath the eye of God, your own master.

When the Apostles returned triumphant after they had preached, healed, and performed all sorts of miracles, see what reward Jesus gave them: "Come apart, and rest a little."[75] In other words: "You have used up much energy; come, regain what you have lost."

And after Pentecost, the Apostles, filled with the Holy Spirit, felt a boundless eagerness to be doing. That is a mark of great souls. When they are in charge of some undertaking, they want to oversee everything and never think they have done enough, so long as there is still something else to do. Thus Moses acted not only as leader and judge of Israel, but as also representative of his people before God. The Lord commanded him, however, to share these offices with other elders. Thus, too, the Apostles cared for the poor, settled differences, preached, and baptized the multitudes. It never occurred to them that, in dividing their time thus between preaching and the service of their neighbor, they had none left for prayer.

That happens to all of us. We are overloaded with work; we might, of course, obtain help, but that hardly ever occurs to us. We must do everything ourselves! It is unwise; we wear ourselves out, and things go no better. We are carried away by the desire for action and self-sacrifice!

[75] Mark 6:31.

But Peter, who, above all the Apostles, was given special light, said one day, "It is not fitting that we do everything; we have no time left for prayer. Let us choose deacons to serve the poor, but we will give our time to prayer and the ministry of the word."[76] Well, who can claim to be holier and more filled with the Holy Spirit than the Apostles? We ought to pray continually day and night!

Virtue that does not have its birth inwardly, beginning in thoughts, affections, and prayer, is not true virtue. Where is the ear of wheat during the winter? It is in the wheat-grain beneath the ground. Warmth and moisture together are needed to make it grow and ripen. Well, now, virtue is a seed planted within you. You can cause it to grow only by prayer, cultivation of the inner life, and sacrifice. The kingdom of God is within you.[77] You will never possess a solid external virtue that is not in the first place internal.

But do you not notice that God's work in us always begins with our inner life? Do you not feel interior temptations? It is God tilling and planting in your heart. Violent tempests will shake the fragile stalk of virtue that is beginning to grow in you and cause it to send out its roots. That is God's work. And when an action costs you an effort, it is not your hand or your body that is resisting, but your too-feeble heart and will.

So you will have no virtues that are not first interior — that do not draw their life from within. How much virtue a soul possesses may be known from the depth of its inner life. This thought ought to be a practical guide for you. When you

[76] Cf. Acts 6:2-4.

[77] Luke 17:21.

make a resolution to practice a certain virtue, resolve to practice it inwardly. Begin, that is, to exercise that virtue in prayer, in habits of thought, in meditation. Later on, you will attain to its outward practice.

It is the course our Lord follows in the Eucharist. Why does He come to us in Communion? To visit us, certainly; but since He remains within us, He still has something else to do there. He comes to implant His virtues in our soul and make them grow, to form Himself in us, to mold us in His image. He comes to accomplish our education in the divine life within us, in such a way that He increases in us as we increase in Him, until we have reached full growth in the perfect man, that is, Himself, Jesus Christ.

Consider the state of Jesus in the Most Blessed Sacrament. Do you see Him there? Yet He is there. Only the angels see His outward life, however. We see nothing of it, and nevertheless we believe that He does live there, as we believe in the sun even when clouds hide it from us, as we believe in the labor of nature although it is entirely imperceptible to our senses. All this is evidence to us that the external life is not the only one, but that there is also an invisible life, a life that is wholly interior, yet very real.

When you receive Communion, therefore, ask our Lord to live in you and let you live in Him. That is something entirely spiritual. It is not what most Christians ask. They receive Communion, but their mind, will, and intention all are abroad seeking external things, so that Jesus finds no one within to entertain Him.

Chapter Eighteen

Be thankful for the gift of the Eucharist

"Thanks be to God for His unspeakable gift."

2 Corinthians 9:15

The most solemn moments of your life are those you spend in thanksgiving, when the King of Heaven and earth, your Savior and your Judge, is yours, fully inclined to grant all you ask of Him.

Devote half an hour, if possible, to this thanksgiving, or, at the very least, fifteen minutes. Rather than abridge your thanksgiving, it would be better, if necessary, to shorten your preparation instead; for there is no more holy, no more salutary, moment for you than when you possess Jesus in your body and in your soul.

The temptation often comes to shorten our thanksgiving. The Devil knows its value, and our nature, our self-love, shrinks from its effects. Determine, therefore, what the duration of your thanksgiving is to be, and never subtract a moment from it without a pressing reason.

Thanksgiving is absolutely necessary if the act of Communion, so holy, is not to degenerate into a mere pious habit. "Be convinced," said St. John Baptist de la Salle[78] to his religious, "that there is in all your life no more precious time than that of Holy Communion and the moments immediately following,

[78] St. John Baptist de la Salle (1651-1719), founder of the Institute of the Brothers of Christian Schools.

during which you have the happiness to be able to speak face-to-face, heart-to-heart, with Jesus."

In the time of thanksgiving, then, the soul finds opportunity to enjoy the Savior, whom it has received and possesses, to pay homage to Him for His love, and to taste at the same time the comforting sweetness of this happy possession. This activity, be assured, is neither a spiritual self-seeking, nor the indulgence of a more or less mystical sensuality; it is the fulfillment of a twofold duty: that which we owe to the divine Host of our Communion, who certainly deserves that we appreciate and enjoy His presence, and that which the soul owes to itself — to find strength and holy joy and gladness in the delights of the richly laden table set forth for it by the heavenly King.

If, after you have received your Savior, you remain unmoved and have no word of thanks to offer Him, you have no heart; you lack all appreciation of what Communion means to you. Perhaps you will protest that you are not of a contemplative nature and are incapable of conversing inwardly. Understand me well! This inward conversation after Communion does not demand a very high degree of spirituality. If you have goodwill, Jesus will speak to you, and you will understand His words, for He speaks the language of the heart, which is understood by all.

Be, then, most faithful where thanksgiving is concerned. The following suggestions will help you derive the fullest benefit from these moments that are so precious to you.

- Having received Jesus and enthroned Him in your heart, remain quiet for a moment, not praying in words, but resting in silent adoration. Like Zacchaeus, like Magdalene, prostrate yourself in spirit with the most holy Virgin at the feet of Jesus. Contemplate Him, while filled with wonder at the sight of His love.

Proclaim Him King of your heart, Spouse of your soul, and hearken to His voice. Say to Him, "Speak, Lord, for Thy servant heareth."[79] Lay your heart at the feet of the heavenly King. Offer your will to execute His commands; consecrate all your senses to His divine service. Bind your intelligence to His throne so that it may nevermore go astray; or rather, lay it beneath His feet so that He may press forth therefrom all pride and vanity.

Do not disturb your soul so long as it is recollected, at peace in the presence of the Lord. In this gentle slumber on the Heart of Jesus, it receives grace, which nourishes it, unites it most sweetly to its Beloved, and profits it more than any other spiritual exercise.

• When this moment is past, begin your thanksgiving, for which you may use with profit the four ends of the Holy Sacrifice:

Adore Jesus, who is enthroned in your heart. Kiss in awe His holy feet and hands. Rest upon His Heart, which burns with love for you. Praise Him for His power. Offer Him your entire being as a sign of your adoration and absolute submission. Proclaim Him your Master, and yourself His happy servant, ready to follow His good pleasure in all things.

Thank Him for having so honored you, so loved you, for having so enriched you in this Holy Communion!

[79] 1 Kings 3:10 (RSV = 1 Sam. 3:10).

Praise His goodness and love for you, who are so poor, and imperfect, and unfaithful. Invite all the angels and saints, the Mother of God also, to bless Him, and praise Him, and thank Him for you. Yes, thank your dear Savior in the thanksgivings of the Blessed Virgin, which were so loving, so perfect.

Be sorry again for all your sins. Weep for them like Magdalene at His feet; repentant love is always tearful, and never thinks it has discharged its debt of gratitude. Make protestation of your faithfulness and love; sacrifice to Him your inordinate affections, your cowardice, your sloth in undertaking anything that calls for self-denial. Entreat of Him the grace never to offend Him again, and beg of Him that you may rather die than commit a deliberate sin.

Ask whatever you will, for now is the moment of grace. Jesus is ready to give you His very kingdom. Indeed, to give Him occasion to bestow His benefits is to give Him pleasure. Pray for the reign of His sanctity in you and in all men. Pray that His charity may fill your heart. Pray for your needs and for all who are dear to you. Pray for your priests, for the Holy Father and his intentions, and for the entire Church. Implore the triumph of Faith, the exaltation of Holy Church, and peace on earth. Ask for holy priests for all peoples, fervent religious, and true adorers of our eucharistic Lord. Implore the spread of the eucharistic reign of Jesus. Pray for the conversion of sinners. Pray for all who have asked your prayers. Finally, pray that Jesus may be known, loved, and served by all mankind.

• Before leaving Him, give an offering of love to your Savior, some sacrifice that you will make for Him during the day.

• During the day, be like an urn that has held a precious perfume, like a saint who has spent one hour in Heaven; do not forget the visit of your King.

The best model for our thanksgiving is Mary receiving the Word in her womb. The most pleasing reception we can make Jesus, and the one best and most rich in graces for us, is to join with His Blessed Mother in adoring Him, present in our hearts.

Without doubt, Mary's adoration in this solemn moment began with an act of deepest humility, for her whole being was overcome by the August majesty of the Word, by the choice it had pleased Him to make of her, His lowly handmaid, and by His unspeakable goodness and love for her and all mankind.

This also must be my first act, my first thought of adoration after Holy Communion. So did Elizabeth receive the Mother of God, who came to her bearing her Savior still hidden in her womb, when she cried out, "Whence is this to me,"[80] this happiness I so little deserve?

Mary's second act was necessarily an expression of joyous thankfulness for God's inexpressible and infinite goodness toward man — an act of humble gratitude that He had chosen His unworthy but only too happy handmaid for His extraordinary favor. Mary's gratitude is breathed forth in acts of love, in acts of praise and blessing; it exalts the divine goodness. For gratitude is all that; it is a great and loving outpouring of the

[80] Luke 1:43.

heart to the one who gives the benefits. Gratitude is the very heart of love.

The third act of the holy Virgin was an act of devotion, the offering and the gift of herself and all her life to the service of God: "Behold the handmaid of the Lord."[81] It was an expression of regret at being and having so little, at her powerlessness to serve Him in a manner corresponding to His worth. She offers herself to serve Him in whatever way He wills and to make every sacrifice He is pleased to demand. Only too happy is she to please Him at this price and respond thus to the love He has shown to men through His Incarnation.

Mary's last act was doubtless one of compassion for poor sinners, for whose salvation the Word became flesh. She knew how to win His infinite mercy in their behalf; she offered herself to make reparation for them, to do penance for them, in order to obtain their pardon and their return to God.

Oh, if I could but adore the Lord as did His good Mother! Like her, I possess Him in Holy Communion.

O my God, give her, who so
adored Thee, to be my true Mother!
Let me share her grace and
her state of continual adoration to the God
she had received in her virginal womb,
that heaven of virtue and love!
I will spend this day in union
with Mary and, like her, live solely
for Jesus present in my heart.

[81] Luke 1:38.

Biographical Note

St. Peter Julian Eymard

(1811-1868)

"In order that . . . storms may not overwhelm you, learn to return frequently to the divine fountainhead to renew your strength and to purify yourself more and more in that torrent of grace and love." The storms of life were not unfamiliar to St. Peter Julian Eymard, who always found in Holy Communion the strength to face them.

Peter Eymard was born in 1811 in La Mure d'Isère, France, and even in his childhood, he showed a great devotion to the Blessed Sacrament. His journey to the priesthood was beset by obstacles, including the strong anticlericalism in the society of his day, his father's reluctance to grant his blessing to Eymard's decision to become a priest, and a serious illness that forced him to leave the novitiate of the Oblates of Mary, which he had entered in 1829. He persevered, however, and was ordained a priest for the Diocese of Grenoble in 1834.

Five years later, Fr. Eymard, who had a fervent devotion to the Blessed Mother, became a member of the Marist Congregation, in which he taught, organized lay societies, and preached eucharistic devotions, such as the Forty Hours Devotion of adoration of the Blessed Sacrament. He was appointed Provincial of the Oblates of Mary in 1845.

In 1857, Fr. Eymard founded the Congregation of the Blessed Sacrament to promote devotion to and adoration of the Eucharist. Despite the struggles involved in the founding of this order — including financial problems and physical exhaustion — he opened his first community in Paris, with himself and one other person as the only members. Soon after a few more men had joined the community, Fr. Eymard was forced to move to another location. A few years later, he was compelled to move again. Because these early communities were so poor, vocations to the order were few. Within about five years, however, Fr. Eymard had attracted enough members to open a regular novitiate, and the order began to spread.

Fr. Eymard also founded the Servants of the Blessed Sacrament, a congregation of cloistered women devoted to perpetual adoration of the Eucharist.

The emphasis on Christ-centered love in his spirituality is evident throughout his writings on the Eucharist. His devotion to the Blessed Sacrament went beyond the worship of the Eucharist to an effort to evangelize those who were estranged from the Church. His numerous writings on the Eucharist echo Christ's tender invitation to receive Him in Communion and present this Sacrament of love as the rest, strength, light, love, peace, joy, and refreshment that every person seeks.

Peter Julian Eymard died in 1868 and was canonized in 1962.

Sophia Institute Press®

Sophia Institute is a nonprofit institution that seeks to restore man's knowledge of eternal truth, including man's knowledge of his own nature, his relation to other persons, and his relation to God. Sophia Institute Press® serves this end in numerous ways: it publishes translations of foreign works to make them accessible for the first time to English-speaking readers; it brings out-of-print books back into print; and it publishes important new books that fulfill the ideals of Sophia Institute. These books afford readers a rich source of the enduring wisdom of mankind.

Sophia Institute Press® makes these high-quality books available to the general public by using advanced technology and by soliciting donations to subsidize its general publishing costs. Your generosity can help Sophia Institute Press® to provide the public with editions of works containing the enduring wisdom of the ages. Please send your tax-deductible contribution to the address below. We also welcome your questions, comments, and suggestions.

For your free catalog, call:

Toll-free: 1-800-888-9344

or write:

Sophia Institute Press® • Box 5284 • Manchester, NH • 03108

or visit our website:

www.sophiainstitute.com

Sophia Institute is a tax-exempt institution as defined by the Internal Revenue Code, Section 501(c)(3). Tax I.D. 22-2548708.